The Dalry Raws

For my sons and grandsons:
Ewan, Callum, Archie, Oliver and Murray

The Dalry Raws

a History of Miners' Accommodation 1848 – 1955

Marie Shevlin

carn

© Marie Shevlin, 2023.
First Published in Great Britain, 2023.

ISBN – 978 1 911043 18 8

Published by Carn Publishing Ltd.,
Lochnoran House,
Auchinleck,
Ayrshire, KA18 3JW.

www.carnpublishing.com

Printed by Bell & Bain Ltd.,
Glasgow, G46 7UQ.

The right of the author to be identified as the author of this work has been asserted by her in accordance with the Copyright, Designs and Patents Act, 1988.

All rights reserved. No part of this publication can be reproduced, stored, or transmitted in any form, or by any means, electronic, mechanical or photocopying, recording or otherwise, without the express written permission of the publisher.

Contents

Preface 7
Introduction 11
A Brief History of Mining Coal and Ironstone in Dalry .. 17
Oral Histories of two Dalry Miners 38
General History of Miners' Raws 46
History of Dalry Raws 51
Oral Histories 88
The Darling Houret Row 133
Conclusion 135
Appendix 1 - Names of householders at Rows, 1885 147
Appendix 2 - Names of householders at Rows, 1948 153
Sources 157
Acknowledgements 160

THE DALRY RAWS

Preface

Like many people, when I retired, I took up genealogy as a hobby. At first I was more interested in my paternal family history as my paternal great grandfather was born on the island of Lismore, spoke Gaelic, and worked as a shepherd. My paternal grandfather was a miner in Lanarkshire who died young of Pneumoconiosis. My father was born in 1924 and brought up in a miners' raw in Carnbroe, Lanarkshire, but moved to Dalry to work at Pencot farm when he was only sixteen.

I had known that my maternal grandfather, Frank Gallacher, had lived in a miners' raw in Dalry when he was young in the late 1890s and early 1900s, but he never discussed it and I never asked him anything about it. When all my grandparents and parents had died I began to be more interested in their early lives and I discovered that most of my ancestors in Dalry had lived in miners' raws as most of the men had been miners. I realised that this must be the case for many Dalry residents. It is not an exaggeration to say that I come from a family of miners, although this has been a recent realisation. Many Dalry residents will have similar ancestry, perhaps, like me, without realising it.

When I started this project I quickly discovered that most people who lived in the miners' rows in Dalry knew them as 'the raws'. This is of course a Scots pronunciation and with respect to their experiences and language, I use this version throughout this project except when quoting from official documents.

A Dalry Mining Family – The Gallacher branch of my family

In the photograph, 'My great grandparents and eight of their children' (on the next page), my great grandfather, Michael Gallacher, was a miner and all five of his sons in the photo also became miners for a time. His father, his brother and three brothers-in-law were also miners. His oldest son, my great uncle Patrick in the centre of the photo, died in a mining accident seven years after the photo was taken.

My great grandmother, Margaret Creily, had three brothers who were miners and three sisters who married miners. Her father and one of her grandfathers had been miners.

Helen married a miner and James had a son who became a miner.

My grandfather, Frank/Francis, married Ellen Curran, the daughter of a miner. Her father, Michael Curran, had died in an explosion in Rosehall Colliery, Coatbridge, Lanarkshire. One of Ellen's grandfathers and at least

My great grandparents and eight of their children: standing rear: Great Uncle John, Great Uncle James; left, Great Grandmother Margaret Creily with Great Uncle Michael on knee, Grandfather Frank, Great Uncle Patrick, Great Aunt Helen, Great Grandfather Michael Gallacher, with Great Aunt Margaret in front. (Three later children, Andrew, Alexander and Susan hadn't been born yet. I estimate this photo was taken around 1903). Photo courtesy of Tom Gallacher.

one uncle had also been miners.

Later in this book I will discuss how a large number of people emigrated from Ireland to Scotland, the men of the family becoming miners. Many of my ancestors were among that number, including the parents of Michael in the group photo and the mother of Margaret. My grandmother, Ellen Curran, had an Irish mother, and all her grandparents were Irish.

On my father's side, his paternal grandparents were Irish but on his mother's side they were all Scottish going back hundreds of years.

Records of the deaths of my great grandfather and great uncle are recorded in the table, 'Records of the deaths of miners in my family' recorded in 'Fatal Accidents in Mines in Scotland'.

A local man who remembered my great uncle Pat's death in a mining accident told my uncle Tom Gallacher, that Pat was brought home from the pit on a horse drawn flat-bed cart. The horse, owned by a local trader, was named Laird of the Hills. My grandfather was fourteen when his older brother, Patrick, died, yet he never mentioned it to me.

No account of mining should omit to mention the large number of men, including my great uncle Patrick Gallacher and great grandfather

THE DALRY RAWS

Records of the deaths of miners in my family recorded in 'Fatal Accidents in Mines in Scotland'

Date	Mine	Area	Owner	Name	Age	Occupation	Cause	Notes
27 January 1910	Blair No. 9	Ayr	Wm. Baird & Co Ltd	Pat Gallacher	19	Miner	Fall of Roof	Fall of roof at road head of working place

Entry from Fatal Accidents in Mines in Scotland – 1910, Scottish Mining Website – My Great Uncle.

Date	Mine	Area	Owner	Name	Age	Occupation	Cause	Notes
26 September 1904	Rosehall No. 14	Lanark	R. Addie & Sons, Collieries Ltd.	Michael Curran	45	Fireman	Explosions of firedamp and coaldust	He stated that when making his morning inspection his safety lamp went out, and that on striking a match to relight it firedamp ignited.

Entry from Fatal Accidents in Mines in Scotland – 1904, Scottish Mining Website – My Great Grandfather.

THE DALRY RAWS

Michael Curran, who lost their lives through this highly dangerous occupation. As often occurred, both Patrick and Michael were not killed immediately but were rescued and died of their injuries shortly afterwards. The Scottish Mining website records the names of 84 Dalry men who died between 1845 and 1930. It would take another book to adequately cover their horrific deaths, often caused by the absence of safety features on machinery and the inherent hazards of extracting rocks from deep underground by hammering or causing explosions. There were also big numbers of miners injured but not killed at work.

'It was estimated in the 1920s that over an average working life of forty years more than a half of all British miners would suffer from a serious disabling injury or contract a chronic life-limiting industrial disease, whilst additionally each miner was liable to suffer on average seven minor disabling "accidents" necessitating more than a week's loss of work. In the 1930s, 80% of all workers in the UK who were classified as long-term disabled (defined as over ten years) by work-related injuries and diseases, were in the mining sector.' A. Turner and A. McArthur in 'The Scottish Historical Review', October 2017.

Ian Terris also makes this point in his memoir, *Twenty Years Down The Mines*, where he describes being involved in, and narrowly missing several small roof falls. Further information on these aspects of mining is covered in some of the books in the list of sources.

Introduction

While investigating my family tree, as well as discovering that most of the men had been miners, I noticed that most of my ancestors' addresses on birth, death and marriage certificates and census forms were miners' raws. For example, the addresses of my great grandparents, Margaret Criely and Michael Gallacher from the old family photograph, are recorded in the following table of addresses of Margaret and Michael Gallacher over their lifetimes.

	Margaret	Michael
Birth	Loans Row	Borestone
1871 census	6 Stoopshill Row	McDonald's Row
1881 census	Wee Peesweep Row	McDonald's Row
1891 census	16 Furnace Row	unknown
Marriage 1892	Peesweep Row	Peesweep Row
Birth of my grandfather 1896	Double Row	Double Row
1901 census	17 Furnace Row	7 Furnace Row
1911 census	11 New Single Row (address when the photo was taken)	
Death	41 Lynn Street (now Vennel Street)	22 Merksworth Avenue

I regret not having asked my father and grandfather more about the raws. I lived for 24 years in the Blair scheme across the road from where the raws had been and I heard neighbours talking about having lived in the raws when they were children before moving to the council houses in the 1950s. I realised that there would probably still be people in their 70s and 80s who might remember their childhood in the raws, so I decided to try to find them and ask them all the questions I hadn't asked my older relatives when they had been alive. I decided to record their answers in an oral history to save these memories for the future and these are recorded in a later section of this book. Many people in Dalry today may not realise that the miners' raws existed, that their ancestors were miners, or that mining was such a large part of their local history; especially since there are very few signs left that mining ever took place in Dalry. It would be a shame if the raws were forgotten. This book is an attempt to avoid that eventuality. Finally, I think it is important to preserve the history of working-class people as their stories are not as well recorded as those of more affluent local residents.

I set out at first to research only the Peesweep Raws, since my ancestors had lived there and I was less interested in Carsehead because there was no family connection there, but people who had lived in Carsehead Raws were also happy to take part in my project. I included these people because their experiences would have been very similar to residents of the Peesweep and their stories deserve to be recorded and preserved for future Dalry residents. I am very happy now that I did include them since their stories are so interesting.

Historical Bits and Pieces

As already mentioned, I had some awareness of mining having been carried out around the Blair area of Dalry and have had conversations with local people about the raws. I found it quite interesting at the time, but now I regret not having asked more questions. These are jottings from memory.

I remember when I was a child, several people still called what was by then the Blair council housing scheme, 'The Peesweep'. I assume these were people who had lived in or visited relatives in the raws before the council houses were built and who still thought of the area as The Peesweep. I was aware of Carsehead Raw still being inhabited in the 1970s, but thought they were agricultural cottages rather than miners' raws.

When cycling the country roads past the Blair in the 1980s, I used to pass a faded notice board stating, 'Caution, lorries turning. Bowertrapping Mine'. This must have been an alternative name for Blair Mine which was situated in the area of Bowertrapping.

At the end of the road from Blairland farm to Blair Road, as an adult I remember iron rails from an old railway being visible in the tarmac of the road and was told it was an old railway used by the mines. I also remember bits of a stone pillar nearby when I was a child. I recently realised that these were the remains of the bridge which took the railway over the road.

A distant relative named Wullie Hodgart used to talk about the raws a lot, named several of them, and was the first person to tell me the story of the Turned Raw having that name because the residents of the Blair Estate had the front doors moved from the front to the back because they didn't like seeing the women sitting on their front doorsteps when they passed on the way to the kirk.

My ex-neighbour, Mary Caig, talked a lot about life in the raws. Her mother had died when Mary was young and it was expected that she would take on the role of keeping house for her father, Dick, who was a miner, and her brother, Gordon. (This is the same Gordon Caig who was Jean Watt Niblock's knight in shining armour as described later in her oral history). I received the impression that they didn't have a wash-house but that may be inaccurate. She definitely talked about getting water for the house from the pump outside which was shared with all the families in the raw. She also talked about the difficulty of washing a miner's working clothes, and even more about how difficult it was to dry them in wet weather when they couldn't be hung out to dry. She described how she often had to call off going out with friends at the weekend because she had to stay in and hold her father's working clothes in front of the fire, turning them frequently but not letting them scorch, to have them ready for him to wear on Monday morning. In fact, at least one romance came to an end when the young man got tired of her calling off arrangements to meet because of her domestic duties. Mary also spoke about how the neighbours in the raws were good to each other. When her mother died, a neighbour was a great support to her and when they were allocated council houses, Mary was very glad to be living in the same terrace as her neighbour from the raws. In fact, I lived in a terrace of six houses and four out of my five neighbours had moved from the raws. Mary told me that when she was a child, she remembers there was a mine almost directly across the road from the north gate at the Blair estate. She remembered the winding gear in the field.

One of my neighbours, Maggie Smith, told me that when she was a child, when the grand folk from the Blair Estate drove by in their pony and trap the weans in the raws would curtsey or salute. She finished this story by saying, 'We didnae ken ony better.'

My uncle Tom Gallacher remembers walking round the Peesweep Raws when he was a child. He said it was a lovely summer day and all the front doors were open. There were a lot of people outside the raws. He had the impression that people generally lived outside a lot.

Local residents referred to the row of houses now named Hillside as 'the Stables' and said that they had originally been single storeyed buildings for the pit ponies and had had a second storey added and been made into terraced houses. The first time they are mentioned as Hillside Cottages in the valuation roll was in 1935, indicating that they had become dwelling houses some time in the previous ten years. In 1855 they appear on a map labelled as 'Stables'.

I have spoken to John Hodgart, son of Wullie Hodgart already mentioned. John was brought up at a smallholding at Wheatyfaulds and never lived in the raws, but he remembers passing the Peesweep Raws and

Old quoits/kites donated by local people, displayed in Dalgarven Mill Museum of Country Life and Costume, Dalgarven, Kilwinning. Photograph author's own with museum's permission.

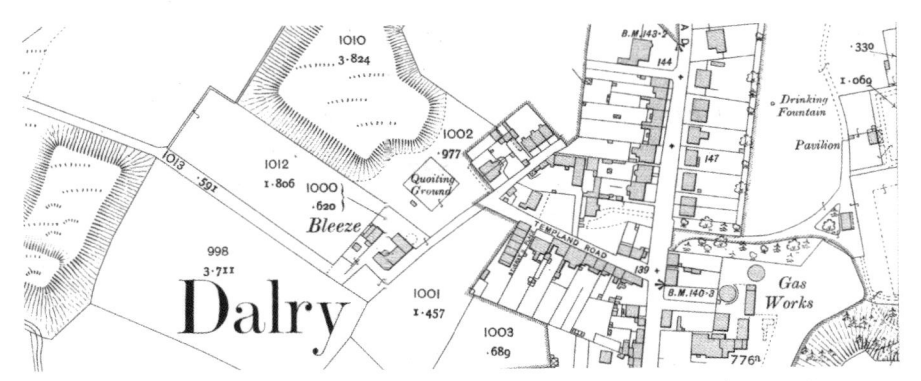

Detail of OS map, Ayrshire XI.3, 25 inches to the mile, published 1910, showing Quoiting (or "Kiting" ground,) reproduced with the permission of the National Library of Scotland.

Stoopshill Raw twice a day on the school bus, and the water pump between the raws and the road. He remembers the stone pillars already mentioned which were part of a bridge carrying the railway over the road. He knew that many of the mines around Dalry were drift mines and locally known as 'in-gaun e'es'. There were numerous small pits including one at Wheatyfaulds. John has many memories of the Den (between Dalry and Beith) and how it used to be much bigger, with a school/church, co-operative shop, police station and two pubs. Miners were very fond of quoiting, pronounced 'kiting', as a pastime. Several quoits or 'kites' are held in Dalgarven Museum and can be seen in the photo, 'Old Quoits.' A quoiting ground is identified in a 1910 map of Dalry above entitled 'Quoiting (or 'Kiting' ground). It was also mentioned on a 1938 map. It may be assumed that kiting was a relatively gentle game of trying to toss a ring over a vertical pole but in fact it was a very energetic game requiring strength to throw the heavy iron kites which could weigh anything from eight up to 23 pounds a distance of 22 yards. The aim was not to throw the kite over the pole but to land nearest to it. Some players placed balls of clay in some of the holes in the kites in an attempt to achieve spin when they threw them.

In the nineteenth and early part of the twentieth century many miners also took part in the sport of curling. Curling rinks were marked on early maps in the public park, near Kersland, and in the private gardens of Linn House. Although not appearing on maps there must have been a rink at Swinridgemuir since a match between the workers of Merry and Cuninghame (miners) and farmers was played for meal for the poor on General Neil's club pond at High Den according to the *Ayr Advertiser* of January 1879.

We discussed the raw at Carsehead called the Sticket Row (discussed later) and John thought of 'The Sticket Minister' by S. R. Crockett. In this

THE DALRY RAWS

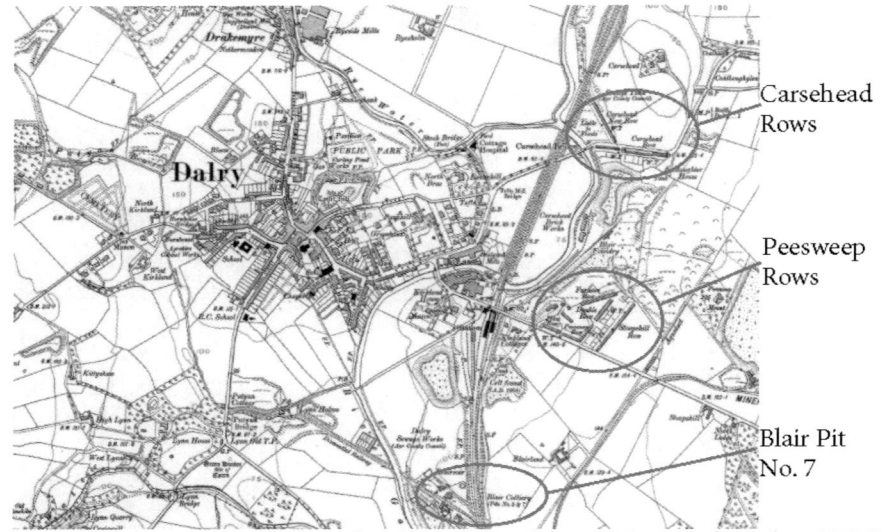

Position of Peesweep and Carsehead raws. Detail from OS Map of Ayrshire XI.NE Survey date 1909, 6 inches to the mile, reproduced with the permission of the National Library of Scotland.

book 'sticket' meant failed but could perhaps also mean unfinished or incomplete.

Peesweep is Scots for a lapwing and in the vicinity of Peesweep Raws there is a low hill called Peesweep Mount, from which Peesweep Raws presumably took their name. Other mining villages had raws or other features named Peesweep including at Auchentiber near Blantyre, Craigbank near Larkhall and Peesweep Brae in Lugar. The construction of the raws was an element in a move towards industrialisation and it is ironic that they were named after such a rural symbol.

Carse in Scots is a 'low and fertile land; generally, that which is adjacent to a river'. A glance at a map of the area around Carsehead Raws will confirm the aptness of this name. Carsehead House nearby existed from around the time of the raws or possibly before the raws.

It takes twenty minutes to walk from the site of Peesweep to Carsehead on the main road, but it is possible to walk from one to the other directly in a much shorter time using a footpath, although the way is very overgrown now. When the raws were occupied this footpath was well used and also gave access from Carsehead to the railway station.

A Brief History of Mining Coal and Ironstone in Dalry

It seems sensible to put the raws in context by briefly describing the development and demise of the mining industry in Dalry parish. Although the village of Dalry was small, the parish covers a much larger area than might be expected. It stretches almost to Largs in the north, Beith in the east, towards Kilwinning in the south and West Kilbride in the west.

Dalry happens to lie in the south-western area of the Scottish coal field, which stretches from the Ayrshire coast to Fife.

This section is not a history of miners and their work, but rather a very brief history of the development and management of the mining industry in Dalry. It would take a whole book to do justice to the skills, hard work, dangers, and exploitation experienced by miners in getting coal and ironstone out of the ground. Several such books have already been written and can be found in the list of sources.

By the time the people who took part in the oral history were living in the raws, mining in Dalry was on its last legs, but the earlier history of the raws was tightly bound up with the history of mining.

Coal was mined much earlier than ironstone in Scotland in general, and Dalry in particular. Monastic records reveal that the monks of Kilwinning Abbey were working coal at 'Monkredding' in the fourteenth century, but coal around Dalry was only worked in a minor way for the next 400 years.

There had been a great expansion of manufacturing and mining in Scotland in the sixteenth and seventeenth centuries, but this passed Ayrshire by as it continued to be a sparsely populated, rural county where people used peat as the main fuel. Coal mining near the coast had developed a little; small amounts being exported to Ireland at this time via the harbours at Ayr, Saltcoats and Irvine. Pits nearest these ports were developed earliest due to the relative ease of transport to the harbours. Places like Dalry, which were further from the ports, were not at first economic to develop because of the associated transport difficulties. Roads were sometimes merely horse tracks, were not well surfaced, and so were totally inadequate for the transportation of heavy goods like coal. (The Glasgow-Ayr railway line through Dalry did not open until 1840.)

Coal had also been used for the industrial production of salt but again the coal was required near the coast, so, for the same reasons of transport difficulties, Dalry was not a feasible source.

The other developing local industry was textiles but this used waterpower rather than coal at that time.

Although the number of formal coal pits was low at this time, farmers would often find a thin seam while digging ditches for drainage and they would dig out the coal for their own use. Despite this, farmers used mainly peat for fuel.

Even where mine owners wanted to expand coal production there was a shortage of labour. In the early years, owners of some Scottish mines partly solved this problem by employing part-time peasant miners who worked the land in summer and mined in winter. I have been unable to confirm if this happened in Dalry but it seems likely. For these reasons, Dalry was later in developing industrial mining.

The 1794 *Statistical Account* states that there were three coal pits within a mile of the village of Dalry. They were between three and 22 fathoms (5.3 to 39.6 metres) deep. (Strictly speaking, a mine allows for access to the coal or ore by a tunnel and a pit allows access by a vertical shaft, but many people use the terms interchangeably.) We cannot know who worked in these early Dalry mines or what were their working conditions, but much is known about the history of mining in Scotland generally at this time. Coal miners in Scotland, and their families, were bound to the colliery in which they worked and to the service of its owner. This bondage was set into law by an Act of Parliament in 1606. Miners were not permitted to leave the employ of their current coal master without his permission and anyone doing so could be forced to return. If a coal master accepted a deserting miner from another mine into his employ he could be fined, and the deserting miner punished. This was a form of serfdom or slavery and was not totally abolished until 1799 when an Act was passed that all colliers in Scotland were 'to be free from their servitude'. Women and children continued to be employed underground until 1842. Thereafter, women and girls were barred from working underground and a minimum age of ten was set for boys to work underground.

The earliest mines had no powered machinery, meaning that all excavation and transport of coal and ore was done by manual labour and the use of dangerous explosives. Coal and ore were carried from the depths to the surface by people, often women, carrying it up ladders in baskets. Installation of steam engines mechanised some of the heavy manual labour by powering 'hutches' to carry workers up and down the shaft and to ferry products from the foot of the shaft to the surface. Movement of men from the base of the shaft to and from the workings was not mechanised and might involve walking or even crawling up to a mile there and back. Likewise, the transport of the coal or ore from where it was dug to the shaft was not mechanised. Hutches full of coal or ore weighing 486lb (220kg) had to be pulled along rails by manpower, later pony power. In this respect, mechanisation had only a limited effect in making mining less arduous.

THE DALRY RAWS

Steam engines improved safety slightly by mechanising ventilation and preventing some explosions and gaseous poisoning, but again the effect was to reduce the incidence of these events, not to eradicate them.

Early exploitation of coal seams was mainly by way of 'in-gaun e'es', (ingoing eyes) whereby tunnels were driven into coal which was outcropping at the surface or close to the surface. It was a very perilous practice due to the danger of falling roofs, build-up of poisonous gases and water accumulation. As well as the danger of poisoning due to the frequent co-existence of coal and gasses like methane, early miners could die from suffocation. This resulted from inadequate ventilation which caused depletion of available oxygen as the miners used it up by breathing. This was exacerbated by an accumulation of carbon dioxide which they breathed out as they worked.

According to the 1826 *Statistical Account*, the number of coal pits in Dalry had increased to six: Kersland, Swinridgemuir, Coalburn, Cleaves, Pitcon and Ryesholm. Coal was now the main domestic fuel but some peat was still burned in the country near the 'mosses' (peat bogs) or as kindling in the town. A map of 1829 records eight coal pits, including Tofts and Barkip, not mentioned in the *Statistical Account*.

Despite the relative economic disadvantage in producing coal away from the coast, by the start of the nineteenth century, the amount of coal exported to Ireland had increased steadily. Some pits further from the coast were able to transport coal to the harbours on newly-built wagonways. For

An old lime kiln near Highfield exposed during construction of the Dalry by-pass section of the A737. It was later demolished. Photo courtesy of Dianne Turner.

example, the Earl of Eglinton exported coal from pits in Kilwinning which was transported to his new harbour in Ardrossan on a wagonway which opened in 1831. Pits and mines away from the coast also started to be developed near lime kilns to provide fuel for lime burning. (Lime was used in construction and the production of fertilisers.) A photo of a disused lime works can be seen in the photo on the previous page.

Near the start of the nineteenth century, ironstone had been discovered near Dalry and coal mining and ironstone mining developed hand in hand for a while. The iron furnaces which produced iron from ore generally used coal, so they greatly increased the local demand. At this time, however, the population of Ayrshire was sparse and the vast majority of men worked the land. Mining was not an attractive industry, to say the least, and coal masters had difficulty recruiting adequate numbers of colliers.

This shortage of labour was overcome by the arrival of large numbers of Irish people escaping the Great Hunger in the 1840s. Since 1819 when a steam packet had started to ply between Belfast and Glasgow or Greenock, calling at Ardrossan, there had been seasonal migration from Ireland to Scotland. People from Ulster used to seek casual agricultural employment in the west of Scotland and occasionally took temporary work in docks and mines and on large civil engineering projects. A trickle of these Irish people would settle in Scotland permanently but during and after the Great Hunger this trickle became a flood.

There appears to have been a flurry of speculation and excavation around Borestone and Swinlees as an 1856 map of the area shows a large number of sites labelled as 'old coal pit' and 'old ironstone pit'. There is also an 'old copper mine'. There were approximately 99 houses in miners' raws at Borestone at that time and 100 at Peesweep and Carsehead combined so it can be seen that for a while the two areas appeared to be equally important in the development of mining in Dalry. The high number of old pits in the area suggests that earlier optimism about finding economically successful pits was ill founded. By 1895 the number of houses had been reduced to 44. By 1909 there were 13 houses in one raw. By 1955 there were none. In this way the early hopes of developing Borestone as a successful mining community appear to have given way to a shift in focus towards Peesweep and Carsehead. The building of the ironworks between Peesweep and Carsehead contributed to the continuation of the raws there as it increased the workforce requiring accommodation in the area.

By 1871 the iron industry was the greatest consumer of coal in Ayrshire. Increasing amounts were also required by brickworks and textile industries which had converted from water-power to coal-driven steam engines. In 1873 there were 22 mines in Dalry according to documents available on the Scottish Mining website but only five were working coal. These were Blair Ironworks mine, Coalheugh Glen, Courthill, Crossroads

THE DALRY RAWS

This image of Pit Number 7, between Dalry and Kilwinning, illustrates the strange juxtaposition of mining and the rural economy in Dalry in the past, photo courtesy of Tom McEwan.

and Swinridgemuir. By 1889 Coalheugh Glen and Courthill had closed according to further records. It is difficult to be definitive about exact dates when mines came into production then closed as records tend to be imprecise. For example, some areas had several numbered pits such as Swinridgemuir 1, 2, 3 and 4 and some records do not make clear to which pit number they are referring. Closed pits were sometimes re-opened, further complicating the issue. For example, there is evidence that between 1873 and 1889 coal pits opened and closed at Bleeze and Middleton at Borestone. The expansion of mining and mechanisation of the textile industry changed Dalry from a rural village to an industrial town. This can be seen in the photograph of Pit Number 7.

Just as the expansion of iron production in Dalry increased the demand for coal, its demise in 1871 (described in the next section) caused coal mining in Dalry to reduce in volume. Nevertheless, there continued to be some demand locally and further afield for coal for domestic use, to power steam locomotives and in industries such as brick manufacture. Since the railway had opened at Dalry in 1840 it was economical to transport coal from Dalry to other areas.

The early twentieth century saw the closure of many local coal mines, some recorded in 'Ayrshire Coalmining and Ancillary Industries' as follows:

Giffen 1 closed in 1900; Kersland 1 & 2 in 1914; Highfield 2 and Swinridgemuir in 1926; Blair 1 – 10 in 1928; Highfield 1 in 1934 and Auchengree 4 in 1936. Muirhouse mine at the Den was still producing coal in 1946. Despite these closures, local census forms and the valuation rolls indicate that a large proportion of men in Dalry continued to work in coal mining until 1940 and beyond.

Many of the oral history interviewees, in a later section, mentioned fathers and grandfathers having been miners and one mentions her husband as a miner.

In 1947 most coal mines were nationalised. Some new drift mines had opened to meet the needs of war-time but they closed in the 1950s.

Local people remember Lochwood still operating in 1952 or later, although strictly speaking it appears to have been in the parish of Kilwinning. The last coal mine to operate in Dalry was Blair 11 and 12 coal mine from 1955 until nearly 1970. The average number of employees was 157 and its peak production was achieved in 1960. Nevertheless, coal production went into sharp decline from the middle of the twentieth century, not just in Dalry but nationally. Some of the factors contributing to this were the Clean Air Act of 1956; the expansion of North Sea oil and gas production; the development of nuclear power stations in preference to coal power and, more recently, concern over coal's role in carbon dioxide emissions and global warming.

As well as these national influences there were local factors, namely, coal had always been difficult to extract in north Ayrshire due to geological faults and igneous intrusions and many of the local mines were worked out. This sounded the death knell for local mining and Blair Mine at Bowertrapping closed in 1969. It is ironic that coal mining ended there because it started very nearby at Swinridgemuir, as already mentioned.

Coincidentally, I visited a working coal mine in the late 1970s. At that time I was working as a Careers Officer and was required to undertake industrial visits to be informed about opportunities and conditions in local places of employment. A team of colleagues and I visited Pennyvenie Colliery in Dalmellington. Although it was under notice of closure, the visit went ahead as it would provide information relevant to other working coal pits.

Although it was one day more than 40 years ago I still remember it clearly as a series of impressions – changing into overalls, helmet, head torch and boots. There were no ladies' size boots and I found the best solution was to wear the safety boots over the canvas shoes I had arrived in. We were led by a manager descending the shaft, travelling towards the coal face on an electric vehicle on rails and stopping half-way through the two-mile journey to switch off our torches to experience the most complete darkness possible. We travelled on for a short distance then dismounted from the vehicle when the manager leading the tour announced that we had arrived at the coal face. I looked around and saw only the walls of the tunnel through which we had been travelling. There was nothing which corresponded with my expectation as to how a coal face would look. The manager then pulled aside a piece of sacking pinned to the wall to reveal a hole around a square metre in area which permitted access to the coal face. We were required to crawl through this. I felt claustrophobic and afraid but logic suggested that the likelihood of my coming to harm was low so I crawled through.

The coal face was less than 1.24m high so we crawled past crouching miners who were using a small coal cutter which operated like a rock drill. This struck the coal wall noisily and forcefully at regular intervals, causing coal lumps to crumble from the coal face. There were three or four miners working on their knees as it was impossible to stand due to the low roof. They shovelled the coal which had been displaced by the coal cutter onto a conveyor belt. We had to crawl over the coal cutter to get to the other side by taking turns to scramble over it on all fours between consecutive blasts.
I saw a miner sitting just outside the coal face eating his piece. I wondered what they did when they needed the toilet as it was an unfeasibly long journey to the nearest plumbed toilet at the surface! There was a works canteen at the surface, but again it was impractical to travel there and back mid shift.

We crossed the conveyor belt carrying the coal to the bottom of the shaft by crawling over a small rickety metal bridge. After we had all crossed safely a huge piece of coal being transported by the conveyor belt knocked over the bridge. The manager replaced the bridge and continued with the tour as if nothing untoward had happened; however, if the bridge had been dislodged while someone was crossing, they would have landed among the coal and been transported on the conveyor belt with no telling what resulting injuries.

As if to reassure us, we were shown the first aid kits set into the wall at regular intervals. They all contained morphine. Specially qualified first aiders in mines were the only people in the UK, apart from doctors, who could legally administer morphine without a prescription. This was obviously provided in case of a serious injury and the requirement for the strongest pain relief.

'Under certain safeguards selected and trained first aid men in the coal mining industry have the privilege of being allowed to use, in an emergency, a preparation of morphia for the alleviation of suffering.

'The drug is available in special ampoule preparation for those first aiders who have been trained in its use, and certified competent for this purpose.

'Normally the drug is held in safes below ground – each safe serving a main man concentration area.'

- First Aid training materials, East Midlands Division, National Coal Board, 1955.

Certificates were awarded to miners on completion of training in administering Morphia.

Returning to the pit head, we had showers and changed into our

> **NATIONAL COAL BOARD—SCOTTISH DIVISION** 10903
> CENTRAL AREA
> Date 10th June, 1965
>
> ## MORPHIA IN MINES SCHEME
>
> I Certify that Mr. J. KERR JR. of ARGYLL Colliery, a qualified First Aid man, has been trained in the use and administration of Morphia and I consider him a suitable person to :—
> (1) administer Morphia
> (2) be in possession of a key to the Morphia safe.
>
> Signed _____ Area Medical Officer
> N.B.—This certificate is valid for 3 years only.
> Part 2 ceases to apply should the worker transfer to another Colliery.

Certificate of training in administration of Morphia in mines. Illustrated with permission of Campbeltown Museum.

own clothes but for a couple of days afterwards I had coal dust in my nose, ears and eyes resulting from even such a short visit. Imagine how much coal dust enters a miner's body over his career.

All the mines in Scotland are now closed, leaving unemployment and enduring deprivation for many ex-miners and their families. A study commissioned by the Coalfields Regeneration Trust in 2019 compared numerous measures of deprivation in former coalfields with the UK as a whole and found that former coalfields had higher levels of all these indicators of deprivation: chronic ill health; unemployment; manual jobs among those working; numbers claiming every type of benefit; and living in social rented houses while also having lower life expectancy; self-employment; earnings of those working and educational attainment level - Beattie & Fothergill, 'The State of the Coalfields 2019'.

IRONSTONE

There are several types of iron ore occurring in Scotland but Blackband Ironstone has always been regarded as the best because it is constituted of both iron ore and carbon. This means that Blackband Ironstone can be smelted in a furnace without the need for adding coal, unlike other types of ore.

The discovery of Blackband Ironstone in Dalry was therefore identified as an excellent investment opportunity for landowners and iron masters.

Iron had been manufactured from ironstone (iron ore) in Scotland from early times using charcoal as fuel, but in 1759 the Carron works in Falkirk was the first to do so economically on a large scale by using coke.

THE DALRY RAWS

The method then spread rapidly throughout the UK.

It was known in 1794 that there was ironstone in various parts of Dalry parish but none of it was being worked. The *Statistical Account* of that date states that there were 2,000 people living in the parish which included the surrounding countryside as well as the village. None, however, were working as ironstone miners. Most were employed in farming or cotton weaving.

The 1836 *Statistical Account* states that a valuable field of ironstone had just been discovered at Blair but meantime the population continued to be employed in agriculture and textiles including weaving. There were about 500 weavers in Dalry at that time and many

Nineteenth-century Ayrshire Embroidery christening robe. Courtesy of Dalgarven Mill Museum of Country Life and Costume, Dalgarven, Kilwinning, Photo by author.

young women and boys were employed in 'Ayrshire Embroidery' - a type of embroidery using white thread on a white background. The floral patterns or 'flowering' was worked at home with materials and orders sent from companies in Glasgow. They were paid, not by the hour, but for the finished garment. When work was plentiful people could earn two shillings (10p) for working 14 to 16 hours a day. Some garments of Ayrshire embroidery held at Dalgarven Museum can be seen in the photo, 'Ayrshire whitework embroidery'. It would be difficult to imagine two more contrasting industries than Ayrshire embroidery with its pristine white materials worked in the light at home and mining black dirty ores hundreds of feet underground in the dark. It must have been a great shock to anyone who transferred from one of the local industries to the other.

Dalry did not however remain a rural village whose residents worked in agriculture or cottage industries for much longer. Several events and situations contributed to the development of ironworking in Dalry including the economic benefits of ironstone and new manufacturing processes already outlined. Just as coal mining had benefitted from the availability of Irish immigrant labour and the development of rail travel, ironstone mining did so too. Finally, the ironstone mines in Lanarkshire which had previously supplied the ore for iron production concentrated in that county were now almost worked out so the ironmasters wanted to identify alternative sources.

It was noted in the geological surveys that the Blackband ironstone seams were between 9 and 20 inches thick (23 and 50 cm) at a depth of 360 feet (110 m). A reasonable bystander would think that it would be impossible to mine but the ironmasters were not deterred, not that they were about to work at extracting the ore themselves. They increased their own wealth by employing low paid workers to do their literal dirty work. The Scottish ironmasters were very happy to provide equipment with little or no safety features and pay men and boys as young as ten a pittance to scrabble underground in dangerous and claustrophobic conditions to extract rocks which would make their employers a fortune.

My grandfather told my uncle that in the 1920s he dug seams 'three quarters of a foot'- (nine inches or 23 cm) thick, lying on his side with a tin sheet jammed above him on the low roof to prevent the water running onto

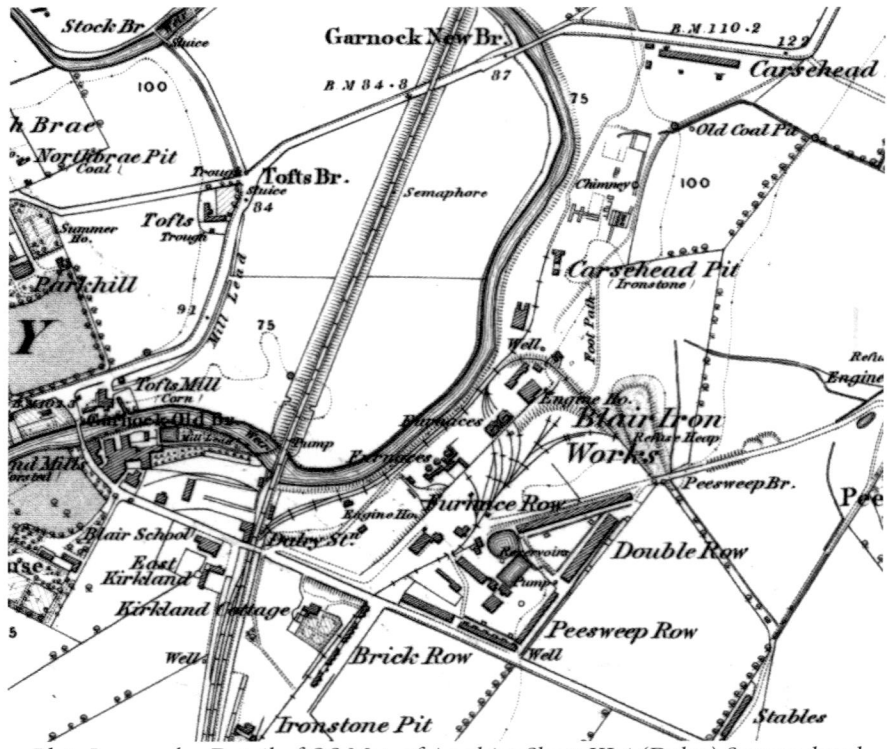

Blair Ironworks. Detail of OS Map of Ayrshire Sheet XI.4 (Dalry) Survey dated 1855, 6 inches to the mile. Reproduced with permission of the National Library of Scotland.

his back. This description of working a nine inch seam is confirmed by the geological surveys mentioned which did indeed state that the Blackband ironstone was sometimes nine inches thick. Needless to say, he advised my uncle not to be a miner when he left school.

The local landowners, Captain William Fortescue Blair of Blair and the Earl of Glasgow, owned the mineral rights and entered into business with a succession of capitalist entrepreneurs who speculated in iron production in Dalry. There was a flurry of local landowners registering the mineral assets associated with their land in the valuation rolls in the nineteenth century but only a handful were lucky enough to be sitting on deposits which could be exploited commercially.

A Glasgow lawyer, John Macdonald, built the Blair Ironworks between Peesweep and Carsehead where smelting began in 1841. This also led to a short-lived increase in coal mining to meet the need for fuel to operate the iron furnaces. The position of the ironworks is recorded in the map opposite.

It was an unusually shaped building and it is strange now to imagine this odd looking building so long ago in its original setting behind Carsehead Raw and down the slope from the Peesweep Raws. An illustration can be seen below.

Fig. 5—CIRCULAR OVENS, BLAIR IRONWORKS, DALRY.

Sourced from "The Engineer" magazine, 20.01.1888, Courtesy of Grace's Guide to British Industrial History.

THE DALRY RAWS

The commencement of iron manufacture in Dalry, however, coincided with a surplus of iron available in Scotland and just over a year later the ironworks ceased operating and fell into the hands of Macdonald's creditors. Just over a year after this the ironworks were bought by Alexander Alison. For a few years the Blair Ironworks operated, producing pig iron, and employing local men and boys. However, Alison speculated unsuccessfully in the railway boom of 1845, was declared bankrupt and Blair Ironworks closed in 1848. It was advertised for sale that year at £65,000, reducing to £50,000 then £45,000. In 1852 the Lanarkshire ironmasters, William Baird & Co bought it for £33,000. The equivalent value today (2023) would be £3,653,254. (https://www.bankofengland.co.uk/monetary-policy/inflation/inflation-calculator)

Transcription of Notice of Sale of Blair Ironworks: Extensive Iron works:

For sale by private bargain

The Blair iron works belonging to the Ayrshire Iron Company, situated in the parish of Dalry and county of Ayr. These works, which have been recently erected at an immense cost, consist of two blowing engines, five blast furnaces, workmen's houses, steam engines for working the minerals, together with utensils at the pits, furnaces etc. all in working order and capable of producing upwards of 35,000 tons of pig iron per annum.

One of the blowing engines, high pressure estimated at 90 horsepower, was erected in 1841; the other, a condensing engine, was erected in 1847, and is estimated at 200 horsepower, the latter being capable of blowing five furnaces, and both fitted up in the most substantial manner, and at present in the best working condition.

The furnaces have been erected with the greatest care, and are fitted with air heating apparatus of the most approved construction. The make of each furnace has generally averaged upwards of 150 tons of iron a week and some of them have produced 180.

There are, besides the manager's house and store buildings, 187 workmen's houses in a habitable state, attached to the furnaces and pits, and there are 20 partly built which could be finished at a small additional outlay. There are also a new foundry, wright shop, fire brick work, smithy etc.

The mineral fields consist of coal, ironstone, limestone and fireclay held in lease by the company at moderate fixed rents and royalties, all situated within easy distance of the furnaces and for the most part have the advantage of railway communication.

The coal fields consist of several hundred acres of which only a small portion has been wrought. Several pits fitted with good engines and machinery are sunk to the coal and partly in operation.

The iron stone consists of the well known black band yielding about

THE DALRY RAWS

3,000 tons of calcined stone per acre and it has been estimated that there are 300 acres or thereby still to work, besides which there is a large extent of clay band ironstone hitherto little wrought but capable of yielding a large output. There are 15 pits with excellent steam engines, some of them in present operation and others ready to resume working.

The limestone quarry is worked by opencast and is connected with the works by railway.

The fireclay is abundant, of excellent quantity and cheaply produced. The Glasgow, Paisley, Kilmarnock and Ayr railway (extending to Carlisle) passes close to and has connection with it, the produce can be conveyed to the city and port of Glasgow (22 miles off) and to the seaports on the Ayrshire coast, each within a few miles of the works. There is a large stock of calcined ironstone, coal and limestone on the ground, so that the works may be put into immediate operation, and under judicious management, the manufacture of pig iron may be carried on to the greatest advantage. The concern will be found to be well worth the attention of persons having the requisite capital and affords an opportunity of entering into the business seldom to be met with.

Malleable Iron works

Considerable progress has been made in the erection of extensive malleable works, which, when completed will be capable of turning out 300 tons of bar iron weekly. The most of the necessary machinery has been prepared by the contractors, and a portion of the work could be brought into operation in a few months to produce the half of the above estimate. This work is nearly adjoining the pig iron works and connected by railway and will be sold either together therewith or separately.

Plans of the property and mineral workings lie for inspection at the Ayrshire Iron Company's office, 113 St Vincent Street, Glasgow, where, on application to Mr Brown, every necessary information will be afforded, and orders given for inspection of the works.'
(Courtesy of British Newspaper Archive)

It is interesting to note that the advertisement mentions '187 houses and 20 partly built'. These must be the raws, newly built or under construction. This is the earliest documentary evidence I have seen for the date of construction of the raws and suggests 1847/8. This total number of 207 houses may include 18 in Kersland Row which was separate from Peesweep and Carsehead and shorter lived, having disappeared by 1915. The next documentary evidence I have seen is the valuation roll of 1855 which provides a rental value of £950 in total but does not itemise or enumerate the houses because they each had a rental value of less than £4 annually. This suggests an estimated minimum number of houses of 238 in 1855. In 1885 when the houses were itemised in the valuation roll there were 210 including Kersland Row, very close to the figure of 207 given in the advertisement.

It is also striking to note that this sales notice of 1848 mentions 15 pits owned by one company whereas 12 years previously the *Statistical Account* stated that there were six collieries and no ironstone pits. This illustrates the speed with which a large number of pits were sunk in the relatively small area of Dalry parish which had previously been almost totally rural.

Who were the Bairds who bought Blair Ironworks from Alexander Alison? Alexander Baird had originally been a farmer in Lanarkshire but he speculated successfully in iron production at Gartsherrie in that county where he and his sons eventually owned 16 blast furnaces manufacturing iron, several coal mines providing fuel for the furnaces, numerous mineral railway lines and a canal to transport goods and finished products. In 1830 he made over the non-agricultural leases he held in the Monklands Iron and Coalfield to five of his eight sons and

James Baird, photo from "The Bairds of Gartsherrie", courtesy of National Library of Scotland

Eglinton Ironworks, Blacklands, Kilwinning, courtesy of North Ayrshire Heritage Centre (Note how close to the 'Airnworks' are the miners' raws.)

established the company, William Baird and Co. One of these sons, James Baird, assumed active management of the business and it was he who expanded the business into Ayrshire. They were so successful that they were regarded as the wealthiest family in Scotland.

The Bairds had turned their attention to Ayrshire as early as 1844 when they bought mineral leases at Swinlees, a site for an ironworks at Kersland and joined the two by a branch railway through Pitcon, although the Kersland Ironworks was never built. They also accepted an offer from the Earl of Eglinton to build the ironworks for him at Blacklands in Kilwinning, beginning operation in 1846.

After the Bairds bought the Blair Ironworks there was a boom in iron production in Dalry but it was short lived, lasting only from 1852 to 1871. Evidence for the impact on Dalry business of the boom in mining and iron production is provided by the 1851-1852 *Post Office Directory*.

This document lists names of local residents, their businesses or occupations (non-manual) and the street of their residence or business. There were still a large number of farmers and several weavers resident in Dalry but the town supported a surprising number of grocers, coal agents, fleshers, tailors, carters, spirit dealers, masons, contractors, bakers, dressmakers, stationers, saddlers, hardware merchants, blacksmiths, tea dealers, shoemakers, innkeepers, a cooper, a watchmaker and a lime merchant. Although the recent influx of miners in the parish were not well paid, presumably the large number each spending a little amounted to enough to boost the local economy.

As ever, the good times passed some people by as evidenced in a report by the Poor Law Commission who visited the parish in 1843. They met 16 people, described as paupers, mostly women who were receiving Poor Law allowance and sometimes financial support from the church session. They were mostly elderly and often widowed. Most but not all of the rooms they were living in were described as small, poorly furnished and dirty.

As already stated the boom was short lived and the reasons for the decline are thought to be: competition from home and overseas; the ironmasters' failure to lead in technical developments; failure to transfer to the new industry of steelmaking; the end of the railway boom of the 1840s; and the better seams of ironstone quickly began to be worked out leaving poorer seams with associated increased production costs, meaning that iron manufacture was no longer so profitable. This decline is clearly illustrated by the decrease in the value of the ironworks according to the valuation rolls at the time, which record the yearly rental value of Blair Ironworks as £1,200 in 1865 and £100 in 1875.

Despite the vicissitudes of investing in iron production, owning the land in which the deposits lay was a profitable business. According

THE DALRY RAWS

Blair House, originally the residence a the Blair family, land and mineral asset owners, photo - author.

to 'Ayrshire Landed Estates in the 19th Century' (J. T. Ward, 1969), local landowner, Captain William Fordyce Blair's annual mineral income between 1851 and 1879 averaged £3406. That amount would be worth £338,028 annually nowadays. This period coincided with an era of expansion and improvement at Blair, presumably at least partly financed by income from mineral rights.

The closure of Blair Ironworks was not a disaster for the Bairds because they had a large share in Kilwinning Ironworks (locally known as the 'airnworks'.) Also nearby was Colville's Ironworks, later steelworks, in Glengarnock, requiring iron ore, so Blackband Ironstone mining continued in Dalry long after the Blair Ironworks closed.

James Baird had built Cambusdoon House in Alloway in 1843 and he used it as a base from which to oversee his interest in ironworks in the south of Ayrshire at Portland, Lugar and Muirkirk.

The opulence of Blair's and Baird's residences contrasts sharply with the inadequacy of the raws where Baird's employees lived. As already mentioned, the Bairds were widely recognised as the richest family in Scotland. James donated £500,000 to the Church of Scotland in 1873. This sum would be worth more than £43,110,959 today. The trust is still in funds today. It was valued at £8 million in 2006. It annually pays out sums of £250,000 or more. He wished the money to be used to 'assist in providing the means of meeting, or, at least, as far as possible promoting, the mitigation of spiritual destitution among the population of Scotland'. (Wikisource, *Dictionary of National Biography*). He did not expend such largesse in mitigating the relative physical destitution of the miners whom

THE DALRY RAWS

Residence of James Baird, Cambusdoon House, Alloway, photo from "The Bairds of Gartsherrie", courtesy of the National Library of Scotland.

he exploited to amass such wealth. Some of that wealth was gained from the value of coal and ironstone brought to the surface by 12-year-old boys and older men who risked, and often lost, life and limb in working underground to make James Baird a rich man. James Baird also endowed many schools, presumably including Blair School in Dalry.

'This School [Blair] is attended by boys and girls of the workmen employed at the Blair Iron Works. The workmen there employed contribute towards the general support of the School. Government allows a small sum but this does not become permanent. The School is regulated by the Master & two assistants who teach Reading, Writing, Arithmetic etc.' (Ordnance Survey Name Book 1855 -1857)

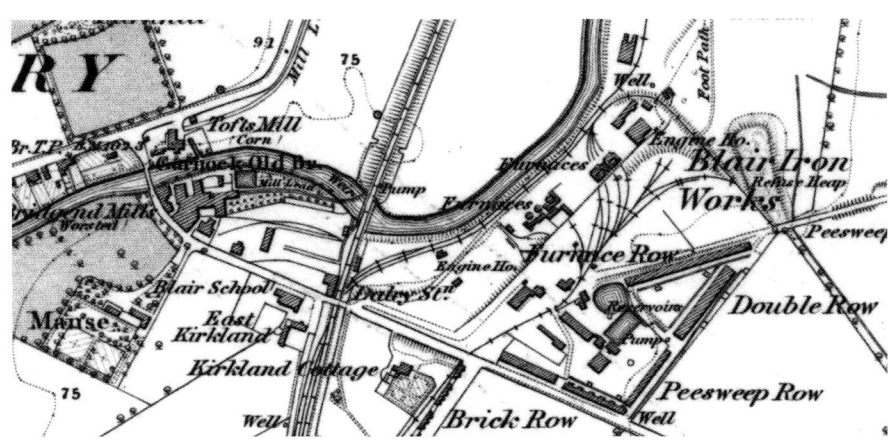

Blair School is found to the left of Dalry Station. Detail of OS Map, Ayrshire Sheet XI.4 (Dalry) 6 inches to the mile, Survey date 1855, Publication date 1857. Reproduced with the permission of the National Library of Scotland.

Among wealthy industrialists at that time schools were valued largely as institutions through which children would receive religious education and thereby develop moral rectitude.

Quotations from various sources in the mid-1840s illustrate this attitude.

'[We are] strongly of the opinion that no plan of education ought to be encouraged in which intellectual instruction is not subordinate to the regulation of the thoughts and habits of the children by the doctrines and precepts of revealed religion'. (Members of the Committee of Council for Education, House of Lords quoted in Maclure [1965].)

'The cause of their apathy, rather plainly ascribes to be, that mental ingenuity was not so much required in their occupations as manual labour'. (Hugh Seymour Tremenheere, Pioneer Inspector of Schools quoted in Bagworth [1998].)

Researchers have reached the same conclusion:

'The Committee emphasised the importance of religious instruction, stressing that it should not be regarded as inferior to intellectual instruction, but in fact superior to it, with religion influencing the teaching of the three Rs. Such an emphasis reflected the opinions of the day, those held by the upper and middle classes, by supporters of early voluntary schools... They believed it was necessary to keep the lower orders of society "under control" and it was generally perceived that this could be achieved by educating them to a sound moral standard. [Some] placed considerable importance on this point, stressing that it contained the main object of the state in elementary education to control the thoughts and habits of the labouring poor.' (Hazel Joy Bagworth in her thesis on the *Development of Elementary Education*, 1998.)

James Baird died in 1876 but the company continued and was managed by other members of the family after his death.

Ironstone mining in Dalry after the closure of the ironworks

In 1873, two years after the ironworks had closed in Dalry, there were still 18 ironstone pits operating at Blair (numbers 1 – 10), Broadlie, Carsehead, Coalheughglen, Crossroads, Davidshill, Flashwood, Greenbank, Hardcraft, Kersland, Kilbirnie, Langlands, Merksworth, Pitcon, Reddance, Ryesholm, Swinridgemuir and Todhills. They obviously had found a market for ironstone outwith Dalry, probably at Glengarnock and Eglinton Ironworks. (It may be puzzling to see a list of Dalry mines including one called 'Kilbirnie'. I believe that this may be due to the mine being nearer Kilbirnie town although in the parish of Dalry. Mention has already been made of the large geographical area covered by Dalry parish and how this area can stray quite near to other towns.)

Some ironstone pits appear to have opened after 1873 at Bleeze,

THE DALRY RAWS

Burn, Muirhouse, Swinlees, Swinridgemuir and Wheatyfauld, but by 1889 all these new pits and several older ones had closed. Yet family census records right up to the most recently available in 1921 show that a large number of Dalry men and boys continued to be employed in the Baird enterprise as colliers and (ironstone) miners, presumably in mines supplying other iron or steelworks. It is difficult to be definitive about which ironstone mines were operating at any particular time for the same reasons given in the discussion of coal mining. By 1895 the ironworks building no longer existed according to the valuation roll of that year. Despite this we know from a document listing abandoned pits that Blair pits 1, 4, 5, 6, 8 and 10 had closed. This implies that pits 2, 3, 7 and 9 were still operational. A foundry was opened at Carsehead around 1875 with William Baird and Company as proprietor and Hugh McCulley as the tenant. This continued in operation until around 1940.

As with coal mining though, there was further closure of ironstone pits in the early twentieth century and by 1928 William Baird and Company had closed all their Blair pits, Numbers 1 – 10 and they closed 12 pits in the Irvine valley between 1918 and 1934.

The Eglinton Ironworks owned by the Earl of Eglinton and William Baird and Company had closed in 1926. Another ironworks which they owned closed in Lugar in 1928. They continued their involvement in steel making in Lanarkshire until the nationalisation of steel manufacture in 1951 when they surprisingly moved into clothing manufacture.

Believed to be Glengarnock Ironworks around 1887, photo courtesy of North Ayrshire Council.

Remains of Pit Number 9 today, where my great uncle Pat was killed at work. These are the only clear remnants of an ironstone and coal pit still in existence in Dalry. Photo courtesy of Robert Barr.

Although the iron industry did continue in Ayrshire in a reduced way, most notably at Glengarnock ironworks, (later steelworks) ironstone mining in Dalry gradually petered out.

Ironstone mining in Dalry was short lived, commencing after coal mining started but finishing before coal mining ceased. As already mentioned, when Blair pit at Bowertrapping closed in 1969 that was the end of mining of any sort in Dalry parish. When they lost their jobs due to closure of their employing mine, many miners transferred to working in the brickworks which had sprung up in Dalry, sometimes using spoil from mining as their raw material.

The end of mining locally and nationally has been a mixed blessing. Working in mining nowadays may be slightly less dangerous than in the past due to modern safety measures, and less arduous due to mechanisation, but it remains extremely hazardous in terms of danger of physical injury or death and it is also detrimental to long-term health due to breathing in

THE DALRY RAWS

toxic particles and chemicals. There are no mine buildings in Dalry now to indicate that in the past there were numerous mines in the area except for ruins at Pit Number 9.

I was lucky enough to make contact with Jock Porter and George Young who worked in Blair Mine as young men, although they never lived in the raws. However, I believe their stories add detail to the history of mining in Dalry as told in the following chapters.

Oral Histories of two Dalry Miners

JOCK PORTER

Jock was born in 1947 in Townend Street and moved to Douglas Avenue in the late 1950s across from the Peesweep Raws which were still occupied. He remembers the Turned Raw and said that the houses were turned away from Blair Road because the people from Blair House did not want to see the washing hanging out when they passed down Blair Road.

Jock's father had been born in a miners' raw at the Den and he worked as a miner near there, then later at Lochend. He remembers that his father had a carbide lamp before battery lamps were common. [These early mining lamps combined calcium carbide and water to produce acetylene which could be lit with a flint and steel to produce a spark. They were hooked onto a hat or helmet and were found to be relatively safe despite the naked flame. However there were a few instances of this type of lamp igniting methane.]

Jock Porter

Jock left school when he was fifteen. The opportunities open to him were Blair Mine, Glengarnock Steelworks or one of the local brickworks, and he applied and was accepted at Blair Mine. He went to Glenburn Pit which was near Prestwick Airport for one week's introductory training then returned to Blair Mine. A short time later he went to Dungavel, near Strathaven (the National Coal Board's Residential Training Centre) where experienced miners taught the trainees skills such as coupling blocks, clipping on hutches, and using a pick. They spent time in the classroom and time underground at Kames Colliery.

When they returned to Blair Mine the trainees' first job was on the surface at the screes. This was where the material that had been mined was sifted and graded. It arrived at the surface in linked hutches. First they were separated then moved onto a tumbler which tipped the hutches over and emptied the contents into the screes. First the screes shook out the dross which was collected separately and could be sold as a fuel to other industries or made into brickettes which could be used domestically. Jock had to remove any rocks which were mixed in with the coal or pieces of coal which were fused with rocks. However, some customers such as ICI at Ardeer liked these coal and rock pieces because they held the heat better. Sometimes the coal was washed. Finally, it was transported off the site by Stevie Brown lorries.

The first underground job which inexperienced miners did was as supply boys. As the name suggests, they provided the materials required by more experienced miners, such as girders and props to hold up the roof and pans and chains which were needed to transport the coal away from the coal face. The materials were loaded into hutches which ran on rails but had to be pulled by rope to where they were needed. On a Friday afternoon at the end of day shift an ice cream van came to the mine and the experienced, better paid miners bought ice cream for their supply boy. Jock started on £4-£5 a week. Jock travelled to Blair Mine in a bus which he could catch either at the Blair scheme or in the town.

Jock explained that Blair Mine was a drift shaft, not a pit so there was no cage. Fifteen to twenty men travelled underground in bogeys on a bogey line. There was one entrance for men and one exit for coal. Each worker going underground was given a token and a duplicate was kept which formed a record of who was underground at any time so that, should an accident occur, it was known if any miners were missing and who they were.

On arriving underground the depute allocated tasks for the day and could occasionally search miners to ensure that they were not taking matches underground as they could cause an explosion.

Blair Mine was wet because water was constantly draining from the surface into the workings. A pump ran continuously to control the water level. There was one main face and the miners who prepared new coal faces were called developers.

After he had worked for only a couple of years at Blair Mine one of Jock's neighbours who was a manager at Douglas's clay mine at Monkredding asked if he would like a job. When he heard that the pay was £20 10s 6d a week he immediately agreed and said that he would start on Monday without working his notice at Blair Mine even though it meant he would lose his 'lying time' from Blair.

The work was harder at the clay mine. Jock pointed out that although it was called clay, they were mining rocks. He had to pull 34 hutches for 200 – 300 yards every shift. Although there was a ventilation system in place to ensure fresh air, there was a low-lying area in the mine where the men knew that carbon dioxide tended to accumulate. One day Jock found himself in this area and became very breathless with his heart thumping. He felt quite panicky and wondered which way he should go to get out of the danger area as quickly as possible. He did manage to run to a safer part of the mine and suffered no long-term ill effects but remembers the experience as very frightening. A bogey line transported the rocks down the hill to the brickworks where they were crushed and made into firebricks which could be used in furnaces. This bogey line could be seen from the A737 road between Dalry and Kilwinning and in fact ran under the road in its route from the mine to the brickworks. Local people still remember seeing the bogeys trundling down the slope when they were travelling past on a bus. The firebricks made at Douglas's brickworks were stronger than construction bricks. Jock worked there from 1962 until it closed in 1980. In fact, Jock was one of the three last miners to leave. One day they were closing the entrances when a fall of material landed on Jock, causing him to fall down a slope and sustain several broken vertebrae. He could not work for two years but once he had recovered he got a job in Roche and worked there until he retired. He said that he liked mining and he worked beside a great bunch of men who all looked out for each other. He talked about how dangerous mining was and how common roof falls were although he also said that safety measures improved over the years. He also talked about mining terminology which was hard for non-miners to understand such as 'snibbles' and 'monkeys' which were different sorts of brakes on hutches.

George Young

George was born in Garnock Street, Dalry in 1947 and the family moved to Kirkland Crescent when he was only a few months old. George had three sisters and one brother. His parents were Hamilton Young and Jeanie King. The family suffered numerous bereavements in a short space of time. His Grandpa died in 1956; one of George's sisters died in 1957; his father in 1958 at the age of 38 and his mother died in 1962 at the age of 44 when George was only 14. His oldest sister, Elizabeth, took care of George and became like a mother to him, although she was only 16½ years old herself at the time. As well as looking after George she became a comptometer operator. George remarked that if it had happened nowadays they would both have been taken into care. They moved to Lynn Avenue from where George was married to Jean Higgins when he was around 20. They had a daughter and a son, but the son died by suicide at the age of 26 so George was bereaved again. All his brothers and sisters are now dead including Elizabeth who died not long before the interview. He still lives in Dalry and has a surviving daughter, two grandsons and a grand-daughter.

George explained that he decided to leave Dalry High School at the earliest opportunity when he was 15. He felt that he had to earn to contribute to the household because his sister was looking after him. This decision was much to the dismay of the head teacher, Mr Holland, because George was in the 'A' class and took Latin, so most of the pupils in that class would stay on at school beyond the minimum leaving age and some would go on to university. George explained that even if his parents had lived he probably would not have stayed on at school because he wasn't interested in sitting national exams and going onto further or higher education. Mr Holland tried to talk George out of the decision, but his mind was made up. He wanted to work in coalmining because it was well paid, especially at

George Young

first. For example, at that time an apprentice joiner would earn £2 17s 6d but a 15-year-old miner's starting wage was £5 5s 6d. However, you had to be 15½ to work in a mine so between leaving school and reaching that age George worked in Harry Gaw's jeweller's shop in Bridgegate, Irvine. As soon as George turned 15½ he started work in Blair Mine. He emphasised that it was a mine, not a pit, because a pit is accessed by a vertical shaft and a lift called a cage, but a mine is accessed by a tunnel. In Blair Mine the men entered the mine by man rider - really just bogeys on rails. This was operated from the wheelhouse where all goods or personnel entering or leaving the mine were controlled. The whereabouts of Blair Mine is recorded in the map on the previous page.

Like all new starts in mining at that time, George was required to attend a three-month course at the National Coal Board's Residential

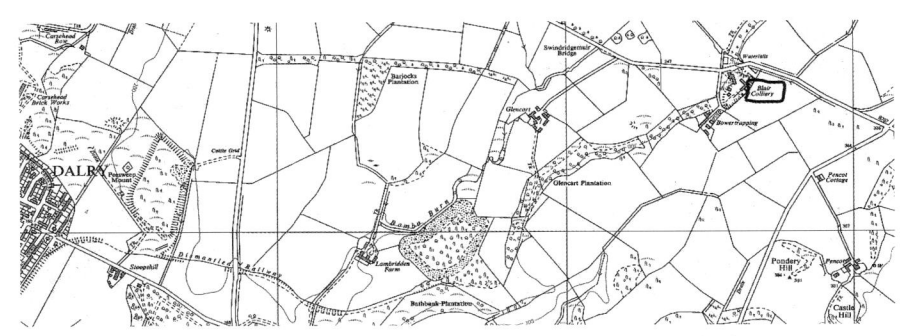

Detail of Ordnance Survey map NS34NW-A, 1:10 000, Published 1958, reproduced with the permission of The National Library of Scotland. Blair mine buildings ringed, Carsehead raws and the Blair council housing scheme are to the west.

Training Centre, at Dungavel, Strathaven. They spent time in the classroom and got practical experience underground at nearby Kames Colliery, Muirkirk. There were around 20 boys from Ayrshire and Lanarkshire there with George, including Owen Gorman also from Dalry. Some boys found the formal lessons difficult but George passed the two Maths tests with 100%, to the surprise of some of the teachers. After completing the residential course he returned to working at Blair Mine. Shortly after this the training officer, Mr Scott, called George into his office and advised George that because he had done so well at Dungavel, he should go to Ayr Technical College to train to be an electrician. George said that he didn't want to do that because the wages working underground were better than apprentice wages. Mr Scott said that the pit manager, Jimmy Kerr, had given him authority to sack George if he didn't agree to go and that he would sack him if he failed the entrance exam. This was to ensure that he didn't subvert the plan by deliberately failing the entrance exam, so he had no choice. Electrician was the most academic apprenticeship. Apprenticeships were also available for fitters but theirs was a less academic course.

George did a four year and three-month apprenticeship while working for the National Coal Board at Blair Mine with day release to Ayr Technical College. When fully qualified his responsibility was to maintain the mining machinery such as coal cutters. There was a transformer at Blair Mine which took electricity from the national grid and transformed the voltage from 11,000 to 3.3.

Because Blair Mine was a few miles outside Dalry, a bus was provided to transport workers to the mine. Other Dalry men George remembers on the bus were John Matthews, John Lyndsay and Jimmy Walker. As well as Dalry men there were men from Dreghorn, Irvine and Kilwinning.

New boys to the work were put on the 'screes' where coal passed by on a conveyor belt on the surface and it was their job to pick out any rocks among the coal. Because it was known that George was more academic than most of the others, the men would tease him, saying, 'We've goat an intellectual wae us the day. Measure thae stanes!'

The first underground job for inexperienced miners was shovelling coal onto the conveyor belt. George knew mining was dangerous but he wasn't scared working underground except when the young boys sometimes played hide and seek with their lamps turned off in total darkness. He said that that was scary. Although the coal face wasn't too far from the entrance they didn't return to the surface for their breaks but ate their pieces underground. Some men chewed tobacco. There were pit head showers and George said that he used them because electricians like him, working underground got just as dirty as the miners. The mine operated on three shifts: night shift from 10pm – 6am, early shift from 6am – 2pm and back shift from 2pm – 10pm.

Night shift was when the coal was 'fired down'. The coal cutter undercut the coal or other harder rock in order to make space for the later explosion. Holes were drilled into the coal and sticks of gelignite inserted using a wooden brush shaft. The front of the hole was packed with sand to contain the explosion. The explosives were fired to dislodge the coal, ready for the early shift workers to move it to the surface.

The early shift was when coal that had been displaced earlier was shovelled onto the conveyor belt, which transported it to a larger conveyor then into hutches which transported it to the surface. The hutches tipped and emptied the coal and other rocks which had been mixed in by mistake onto the screes. These were like huge riddles which sorted the coal by size. The back shift was when new underground roadways were prepared to allow access to new coal, the coal cutter and additional props to hold up the roof were positioned.

They used the retreating longwall method whereby two parallel roadways (tunnels) were driven to the furthest extent of the coal face. A third roadway joined the original two at right angles. This became the coal face. The coal was then stripped from that part of the coal face using coal cutters and hydraulic supports called doughties were placed to hold the roof up. When all the coal had been removed from that area the machinery was moved back towards the entrance (retreating) and when the machinery with roof supports was removed the cavity eventually caved in, sometimes almost straight away and sometimes not for some time afterwards. Underground workers could hear the cavity which had been stripped of coal and was threatening to cave in creaking regularly until it eventually crashed down with a deafening noise. Some doughties were left to prevent the access tunnels and new coal face from falling in. So long as you were behind the doughty support you were safe but one miner who was very devoutly religious was so frightened by the noise of the roof falling in, he didn't feel safe even behind the doughty and he ran away swearing, the only time they ever heard him swear. They were supplied with overalls, steel toe capped boots and helmets. Even when wearing a helmet if you hit your head off a girder you could give yourself a concussion. Miners had to buy their own picks. They did not have ear defenders.

George remembers one fatal accident in the mine when a young man from Kilwinning was crushed between two hutches of coal due to not engaging the safety mechanism which was meant to prevent them getting close enough to crush someone who got between them. Because of the dangerous nature of the work, miners worked very well together and got on well. An emergency might occur at any time when you would have to depend on your work mates for help. George joked that if two miners had a disagreement they would go up to the yard together, one would come back with a black eye and that would be the disagreement settled.

THE DALRY RAWS

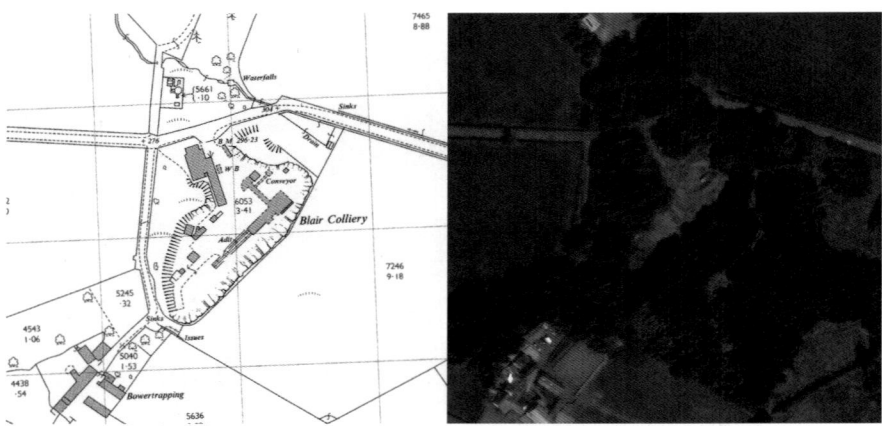

Detail of Ordnance Survey map NS34NW-A, 1:10 000, Published 1958, reproduced with the permission of The National Library of Scotland, showing Blair Mine at Bowertrapping, side by side with modern Microsoft Bing satellite image. Microsoft product screen shot reprinted with permission from Microsoft Corporation.

Mining was an unhealthy occupation. George's father-in-law who worked in Douglas Fireclay Mine developed Pneumoconiosis.

The coalface at Blair was a reasonable height, around five feet, so although the men had to stoop it was much easier to work there than some other mines. George occasionally visited other mines and knew that at Lochwood, on the back road to Saltcoats, for example, the men were crawling around in water. He also visited Barony Mine and the men there asked him, 'Whit pit dae ye work at, son?' The men were wags and when he said that he came from Blair Mine the Barony men said, 'Oh the tatty pit? We heard the roof fell in last week and there was naethin but tatties and turnips fell doon.' This was their way of teasing because Blair Mine was only 500 feet (152metres) deep while Barony was 2,000 feet (609 metres) deep. The gradient into Blair Mine was 1:3 so the entrance tunnel must have been about 1,580 feet (480 metres) long. George used to exit up the slope on foot to increase his fitness. He played football for Rye Rovers and Dalry Thistle in his spare time. He also played for the Scottish Miners versus the Welsh Miners at a Miners' Gala-day at Holyrood Park in the late 1960s. The score was 2-1 to Scotland and George scored the first goal.

When Blair Mine closed, being considered uneconomic, George had the opportunity to transfer to Lady Victoria Colliery at Newtongrange, Midlothian, now the site of the Scottish Mining Museum but he didn't want to move away from Dalry. He also had the opportunity to work as a 'spark' at Douglas brickworks but in the end he moved to working at electrical maintenance at ICI where his wife worked. He was unhappy there because he was earning less than his wife so when, after three years there, he got the chance to move to Roche he was glad to do so. He worked there until he retired and liked it very much at first, but it became a drudge and he was glad to retire.

George said that the best time of his life was down the pits and that, by and large, miners were the finest group of men he ever worked with.

He said that the last time he had been to the site of the mine there was nothing left of the mine buildings and it had been turned into a picnic site. The map comparing a detail from a 1958 map of Blair mine with a present day photo illustrates how all signs of an industrial area can disappear.

Note: Online records from Railscot.co.uk and Mindat.org allocate different names to Blair pit; sometimes it is called 'Blair b mine' and sometimes 'Blair 11 and 12'. It operated from 1953 to 1969. 'Blair a mine' seems to have been an alternative name for Pit Number 9.

General History of Miners' Raws

Raws were always built close to the mine or ironworks where the inhabitants were employed. (This can be seen in the earlier photograph of Eglinton Ironworks.) Aspects of the inhabitants' comfort such as good drainage or protection from prevailing weather were never considered. When raws were built, it was never known for how long the mines or pits they served would last or for how long the raws would be required. This mitigated against spending money on good construction and resulted in the provision of the most basic of accommodation. ('The Iron Industry in Ayrshire', R. H. Campbell.)

It has been already mentioned how in the very early years of the industry, miners were held in bondage and had no right to choose their own place of work or residence. Even after this was abolished, the attitude persisted that miners' houses were really a part of their wages and should be rent free or very cheap to rent as they were 'tied houses'. This was perhaps reinforced by the eviction of widows and children if the head of the household died, a practice which continued into the twentieth century. Until the later decline of the mining industry, in many areas the houses were largely regarded as pieces of mining plant, not as places of free tenancy. This led to the tenants' ambivalence about their housing. For example, in the 1913 Housing Report it was reported that tenants were often hesitant about complaining about shortcomings which were clear for all to see because they feared repercussions such as eviction or large increases in rents to pay for improvements.

A paper presented to Largs Local History Society by John Miller describes how there was no internal water supply in any of the houses, no toilet, and bathrooms were completely unknown. Cold water was brought into the house in an enamel bucket filled from the tap at the pump or in the wash house and hot water was obtained by boiling a kettle on the open fire or range. Washing up after a meal was carried out in a basin on the table. The wastewater was carried outside and disposed of down the storm drain. Lighting was chiefly by paraffin lamp although in some cases the houses had gas light. In many cases, street lighting was provided only a short time before the raws were demolished.

Royal Commission on housing conditions of the Industrial Population of Scotland, rural & urban, 1918

The Ayrshire Miners Union had been formed in 1886 with James Keir

THE DALRY RAWS

Hardie (1856-1915) as organising secretary. (Hardie, born in Lanarkshire, worked in mines from age 10, later became a trade unionist, founder of the Labour Party, a Member of Parliament and Labour's first parliamentary leader from 1906 to 1908. He had visited Dalry in 1883.) Recognising the detrimental effect of miners' raws on the health of its members, the union agitated and achieved agreement to a Royal Commission on Housing in Scotland.

In 1913 it began gathering evidence by visiting a large number of miners' raws in Scotland including those at Peesweep and Carsehead. Evidence presented to the Commission described conditions in miners' rows in general and also detailed many of the raws they sampled.

The report presented to the Commission in 1918, after the interruption of the First World War, found that miners' houses were almost universally built of the cheapest available materials and arranged in the cheapest form, namely the long, straight row. This was less expensive than separate houses each requiring their own gable ends. They were built of brick or stone with roofs of thatch, slate, or tar cloth. They opened on to a private roadway for cart traffic, with a surface channel for drainage which was usually wholly inadequate so that the ground directly outside the houses was either dry and dusty or wet and muddy. In dry weather dust from coal or iron ore permeated the air and entered the houses. There were outside water pumps, dry closets for toilets shared by several families, and sometimes wash-houses. The dry closets tended to be positioned in the most conspicuous places and it was reported that in hot weather swarms of flies from the dry closets entered the houses in some miners' villages. In many cases the dry closets were double without a dividing wall or door, showing that the designers expected residents to relieve themselves in the presence of a neighbour. Sometimes there were small gardens or clothes drying greens on the further side of the outhouses. It was noted that badly selected sites often threw real difficulties in the way of improvements of sanitation by making satisfactory drainage difficult.

Evidence was also presented that in many cases the only outlook of the raws was onto the 'bings' (refuse heaps) of the pit at which the men found employment, old obsolete properties, workshops and water reservoirs. This description makes me realise that to live in a miners' raw at that time was to live on the outskirts of a heavy industrial site, looking onto a scarred industrial landscape with the concomitant noisy, dirty atmosphere.

The reporters to the Commission described common features in miners' villages which pertained in Dalry such as back-to-back or double rows which reduced the number of windows in each property and, just as the long, straight rows saved building separate gable ends, the double row halved the number of back walls required. They were either single-ends or room and kitchens with set-in beds, supplemented by hurleys (beds on

THE DALRY RAWS

wheels which could be pulled out when needed at night and wheeled out of the way during the day.) Crowded conditions were normal in almost every raw; subsidence and disrepair common; facilities primitive. Coal houses were rarely provided - so fuel was often stored on the bare earth under the set-in beds. Where wash houses had not been provided, clothes (and miners) had to be washed in bines (tin tubs) indoors on the brick tile floors. The conclusions, as reported to the Liberal Government of the time, were that the 'only remedy was a Closing Order on the great bulk of the houses. Employers should not be the house owners.'

The report found that Public Health Acts of 1848 and 1875 were not being implemented by County Councils. They were castigated as failures because they had not implemented the requirements of the 1848 Public Health Act, namely improved drainage, and provision of sewers; the removal of all refuse from houses, streets, and roads; the provision of clean drinking water and the appointment of a medical officer for each town.

The intention of the 1875 Act was to make the provisions of the earlier Act compulsory and with the Artisans' and Labourers' Dwellings Improvement Act 1875, house owners had become responsible for keeping their properties in good order. It also allowed the local authorities to purchase and demolish any dwelling that was not improved, but the Acts were found to be rarely, if ever, implemented. The report to the Commission suspected that the reason was that, in many cases, the owners of the unfit houses were county councillors, and that the sanitary inspectors did not desire to offend the men whom they regarded as their employers by compelling them to conform to the Public Health Acts.

It was recognised that it would be unwise to close the existing houses until new houses were built, but the authors of the report suggested that the owners of the existing houses should be compelled, until new houses were built, to ensure that every house ought to have a wooden floor and a cement pavement in front of it. Each family was to be provided with a coalhouse and a closet, and there should be at least one washing house for every three tenants. Every ashpit should be swept away at once, and each family provided with a metal dustbin which should be emptied every morning. Legislation should be passed prohibiting the building of any houses for workmen's dwellings of smaller dimensions than three rooms, scullery, and bathroom, with water closet and coalhouse attached.

(The oral histories indicate that of all these requirements, the only one implemented by the time the raws in Dalry were demolished in the 1950s, was the provision of water closets and metal dustbins.)

The First World War had postponed the implementation of the Royal Commission's work. Tenants continued to live in raws with the same faults which had long been identified until at last in the 1920s a sequence of Acts of Parliament facilitated the expansion of local authority housing and

THE DALRY RAWS

commenced the transfer of tenants out of the raws throughout Scotland. These acts were largely due to the leadership of John Wheatley who was a leader of the 'Red Clydeside' group of Labour MPs in the 1920s. He was a key figure in the development of housing policy in the UK, and the architect of the 1924 Housing Act. His concern about housing stemmed from his own impoverished background as the son of an Irish miner in the Lanarkshire coalfields. Wheatley himself went down the pits at age 12 and lived in a single end with his eight brothers and sisters, parents, and lodgers. The children all slept together in a hurley bed. There was only a communal toilet and water had to be hauled from a common tap.

Wheatley managed to escape the pits through self-education and eventually became a successful businessman. He entered politics as a councillor for Shettleston, later becoming leader of the Labour group on the City Council. Wheatley argued that only the government could supply the answer to the housing problem by building reasonably priced housing for workers. In 1922 he was elected to Parliament, and in 1924 he had a chance to put his ideas into practice when he was appointed Minister of Health in the first Labour government. This government implemented a large council house building programme of which Dalry benefitted with the building of council flats in Townend Street, Garnock Street, Lynn Avenue and Merksworth Avenue. It is largely thanks to him that some of the residents of the raws were eventually able to move into brand new council flats with indoor plumbing, electricity, private toilets and baths, several bedrooms separate from the living accommodation and removal of overcrowding. For this reason, these houses were locally called 'Wheatley' houses. They are still in use today – a testament to the quality of the build and materials used almost 100 years ago.

Although the 1920s saw the first council houses built, scarcity of public money hindered slum clearance and reduction of overcrowding on the scale required. It must be remembered that miners' raws were not the only type of substandard housing occupied by the working classes. Residents of tenements in towns and cities experienced similar overcrowding and insufficient amenities as the miners and their families. There were further delays during and immediately after the Second World War when building was virtually halted. Furthermore, the failure to close uninhabitable houses frequently rested on the allegation that the life of the mine was about to end, and that the houses would soon become automatically surplus to requirements. In some areas the life of the mine did end; but the houses were transferred to other owners and so the miners' raws continued in use while local authorities gradually increased their provision of council houses.

It was not until the 1950s that enough council houses eventually became available to re-house all remaining tenants in the raws. This was nearly half a century after the 1913 Report was compiled and at last, most of the miners' raws in Scotland were demolished.

History of Dalry Raws

This chapter deals with the building, ownership, and development of the raws. Further information on what it was like to live in Carsehead and Peesweep Raws in living memory is given in the oral histories. The main focus of this project is life in Carsehead and Peesweep Raws but there were many other raws in Dalry Parish in the past as itemised in the map showing the position of the raws and the table of the number of houses in the raws. Evidence for their existence has been found in census returns or maps. Some were small raws with only a few houses while Borestone had 97 houses. It has been impossible to ascertain the exact date of building or demolition of all the raws but suffice it to say that Peesweep and Carsehead Raws were last to be demolished.

Because of the large scale on the 25 inches to the mile map of 1855 it is possible to count the number of individual houses in the raws as recorded in the following table:

Row	Number of houses
Blair Row	Estimate 4
Borestone	97
Brick Row	12
Burn Row	6
Carsehead	11 in 1855, (69 in 1905 and 32 in 1913)
The Den	69
Kersland	18
Linn	4
Little Acre / Creepies	7
Loans	4
Park Terrace	25
Patrick's Row	5
Peesweep Raws	90
Riddens	Estimate 8
Swinlees	Estimate 20
Total	Estimate 380

Later in this chapter I estimate the average number of people living in each house as 5.4 so it is likely that 2,052 people in the Parish of Dalry were living in miners' raws, although we can't be sure they were all occupied at the same time.

THE DALRY RAWS

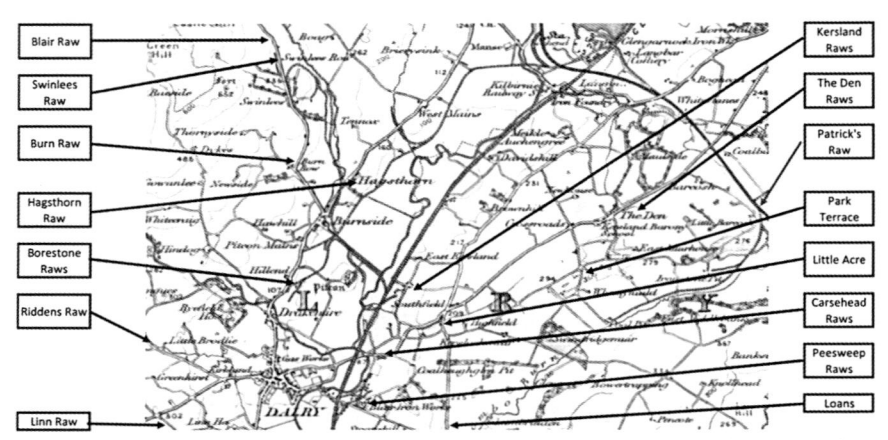

Detail of OS Map, Ayrshire Sheet 22 (Kilmarnock)1 inch to the mile, survey date c. 1855, reproduced with the permission of The National Library of Scotland.

A map of Dalry parish by Robert Aitken in 1829 shows the town of Dalry with six streets: Main Street, New Street, North Street, Courthill Street, The Vennel and Sharon Street. There are coal pits at Hardcroft, Hawhill, Tofts, Wheatyfaulds and Highfield. Between 1850 and 1895 when mining and ironworking were booming, Aitken Street, Garnock Street, James Street, Queen Street (later renamed Townend Street), Templeland Road (later Templand Road) and West End were established.

Borestone and Swinlees to the north of Dalry and the Den to the east were initially significant mining areas and by 1856 raws in these areas as well as Peesweep and Carsehead appeared on maps. Over time many raws disappeared from old maps, sometimes doing so gradually as raws in each area reduced in number until eventually the last one disappeared. The reason for the earlier abandonment and demolition of the raws other than Peesweep and Carsehead was probably due to the earlier closure of the pits they served.

We do know that the focus of mining and iron manufacture in Dalry moved to the area near Peesweep and Carsehead in the second half of the nineteenth century and eventually the raws there became the only ones still occupied in Dalry. Of the others, The Den seems to have been the area with raws which survived the longest. Although I have not been able to find anyone who lived in the Den, some local people know that their parents or grandparents lived there. According to the valuation rolls the raws there seem to have been demolished, or at least ceased to be occupied, some time between 1935 and 1940.

There appear to be very few photographs of the raws in Dalry in existence and only three of the respondents in the oral histories had any photographs, but an appeal on Dalry Facebook pages resulted in the Thompson and Sweeney families providing these photographs.

THE DALRY RAWS

The Thompson family outside Little Acre; Lizzie, Agnes, Robert, Belle, Isabella (McCalmont), Jenny. There were five older children not in the photo. Photo courtesy of Irene Beadle.

The Thompson family house at Little Acre Raw also known as the Creepies. Photo courtesy of Irene Beadle.

THE DALRY RAWS

A group of residents outside Patrick Raw, adults left to right:
Willie Allan, Jessie Gilbert, Unknown, Mrs Maggie King, Unknown, Mrs Allan
Photo courtesy of the Sweeney family.
Photo enhanced by Hugh Anderson.

HISTORY OF PEESWEEP AND CARSEHEAD

The following information has been gleaned from historical records such as valuations rolls, censuses, maps and the document, 'Ayrshire Miners' Rows - Evidence submitted to the Royal Commission On Housing In Scotland' by J Brown and T McKerrell from 1913. I believe it is the first time that this information has been amalgamated in this way.

The Bairds and other mine owners had experience of supplying housing for miners in Lanarkshire and they transferred the same model to Peesweep and Carsehead.

Although raws were often built outside existing towns, Carsehead and Peesweep were not so isolated as some other local raws such as Swinlees had been. In other parts of Ayrshire, such as Benquhat, Burnfoothill, Lethanhill, Darnconner and Commondyke, raws were even more isolated. The difference was that in Dalry the coal and iron ore deposits were found near the village of Dalry, allowing for miners to walk to the pits and mines from the town. In other parts of Ayrshire the deposits were found in unpopulated areas, too far away from existing towns to allow miners to walk to work each day. This necessitated the building of miners' villages near the mines but far from existing towns. This also explains why the isolated villages were never built over as the only reason for living there was to work in the mines. In contrast, when Peesweep raws were no longer required or fit for human habitation, they were demolished and built over with housing for people who found it convenient to live in the town of

THE DALRY RAWS

The "Creepies" or Little Acre, photo courtesy of the Pollacchi Family.

Dalry with its shops, amenities and other sources of employment.

When Carsehead and Peesweep were built on the outskirts of the town, Dalry consisted of only six streets, already mentioned and the newly built raws were separated from these by quite a long uninhabited road although it is now the populated areas of the end of New Street and Blair Road.

Although the raws in Dalry were built on what must have originally been pleasant rural surroundings, the industrialisation of the areas nearby resulted in the raws being dominated by pit buildings, shafts, waste heaps, mineral railways, and main rail lines slightly further away. This was common especially in Lanarkshire and Ayrshire.

Naming the raws

Investigating records of the raws soon revealed that the names of individual raws seemed to change over time or depending on the record consulted. For example, I noticed that New Single Row does not appear on any map and Stoopshill Row does not appear in any early valuation roll. It was at first confusing trying to follow one raw through time because some changed their names in this way.

Fortunately each raw had a unique number of houses which did not alter over time (except towards the end of their existence when demolition started) so it became possible to find a raw by its number of housing units in various documents and note how its name may have changed. These

THE DALRY RAWS

findings are summarised in the table below:

Number of houses	1855 map large scale	1885 valuation roll	1895 map large scale	1895 & 1905 valuation rolls	1913 housing commission report	1915 & 1925 valuation rolls	1935 valuation rolls	1940 valuation roll	Notes
11	Not named	Foreman's (11)	Not named	Foreman's (11)	Front (11)	Foreman's (11)	Foreman's (11)	Foreman's (11)	Dandy Row 1891 Census
23	Furnace (23)	Furnace (22)	Furnace (23)	Furnace (23)	Furnace (23)	Furnace (23)	Furnace (23)	Furnace (23)	
24	Peesweep (12+12)	Peesweep (24)	Peesweep (24)	Peesweep (24)	Turned Row + Wee Row (22) + 2 for reading room	Peesweep (12) + 2 for reading room	Peesweep (12)	Peesweep (11)	Reduction in number due to demolition of 'Wee Raw'
32	Double (32)	Single (32)	Double (32)	New Single (32)	Double	New Single (31)	New Single (31)	New Single (31)	
34	Not yet built	Double (34)	Stoopshill (34)	New Double (34)	Stoopshill (24)	New Double (22)	New Double (21)	New Double (18)	Reduction in number due to demolition

56

THE DALRY RAWS

FURNACE ROW
This raw was nearest to the ironworks.

FRONT/FOREMAN'S/DANDY ROW
Many villages of miners' raws had a raw named 'Foreman's Row'. Raws with this name were generally of a higher standard than the others and usually the foremen or 'oversmen' were housed there. Foreman's Raw in the Peesweep was the only raw in 1913 identified as having wash houses so this might indicate that it consisted of better accommodation. The fact that it was sometimes called 'Dandy Raw' in the early years also suggests that it may have been superior to others nearby.

PEESWEEP/WEE/TURNED ROW
Sometimes 'Peesweep' was used to describe the whole collection of raws off Blair Road and sometimes it applied to only one raw. This raw started with 24 houses but, as later explained, two houses were converted into the reading room. (Recorded in valuation rolls 1905 – 1930.) The valuation rolls and large scale maps continued to record 24 units, no matter their use. However, the Housing Commission in 1913 were only interested in the buildings which were used as houses so they reported on 22, ignoring the reading room which had no-one resident.

The large scale map, 'Map with individual houses outlined – Peesweep' reveals that this raw actually consisted of two raws at 90 degrees to each other with a small gap between. The members of the Housing Commission who visited in 1913 recorded these raws as 'Turned Row' and 'Wee Row', presumably because the residents to whom they spoke named them thus. Wee Row appears to have been the raw at right angles to Blair Road. They were single ends and had no porches so would have appeared smaller than Turned Row although they were also single ends. The commission reported that the floors were 18 inches below the surface of the road with consequent dampness and occasional flooding. Between 1913 and 1915, 12 houses were demolished in Peesweep Raw. The map 'Comparing aerial photograph 1944 with map 1895, Peesweep' reveals that in fact the part designated Wee Row was demolished.

Turned Row ran parallel to Blair Road and the two end houses (before the turn into Wee Row) became the Reading Room, although its official address was 11 & 12 Peesweep Row.

The name, 'Turned Row' refers to the fact that their front doors were turned away from the main thoroughfare of Blair Road, unlike Front/Foreman's Row which faced onto the road. It can be imagined that it might have looked quite strange to see the back of the houses from the road and that local people would seek an explanation for this oddity.

Earlier I recounted the commonly held understanding in Dalry that the residents of Blair House had insisted on having the doorways removed from the front and replaced to the back so that they would not be offended by seeing the tenants going about their business at their only door. I knew this story before I started this project, several of the oral history respondents repeated it and other people who never lived in the raws have mentioned it to me when they heard that I was writing about the raws, so it is a widely and strongly held local belief.

However, in the course of researching this history I have come to doubt the story for the following reasons: if the residents of Blair House had the front doors removed and replaced to the other side of the house in this raw, why not also in adjacent Foreman's/Front Raw? It was common practice all over Scotland in planning raws that where they were built in a square the front doors all faced inwards to the square. At Peesweep the raws formed a triangle shape and I believe that the front doors would have faced inwards to the triangle from when they were first built. The exception is Foreman's/Front Raw which had doors facing away from the triangle. This could have been part of the efforts to make them of a better standard and more desirable.

Although I have reached this conclusion, the story of Turned Raw is so ingrained in the local belief system that I don't expect to change many people's minds! R. H. Campbell did refer to an instance of doors and windows being altered in 'The Iron Industry of Ayrshire'. In discussing the owners' attitudes to miners' houses he states. 'One row in Ayrshire had all its windows and doors reversed after construction to prevent idle glances at the laird going from the station to his house.' He does not mention which town or area in which this occurred and it is impossible to say whether it is a true account of something that happened or whether it is an urban myth.

DOUBLE/SINGLE/NEW SINGLE ROW
The table, 'Naming the Raws – Peesweep' reveals that this raw changed its name between three alternatives several times, being variously known as Double Row, Single Row and New Single Row. Double Row is descriptive of the back to back construction and Single perhaps relates to the houses being single ends. I suspect that it acquired the title New Single Row when New Double Row (also known as Stoopshill) was built in order to differentiate the two. It is strange to think of it acquiring the description 'New' when it was 40 years old.

STOOPSHILL/DOUBLE/NEW DOUBLE ROW
Presumably the name Stoopshill was used in maps and the Housing Commission report because it was nearest to Stoopshill farm. Where it was called Double Row, that probably refers to the fact that the houses were room and kitchens. In fact, there were extra subdivisions of the rooms

THE DALRY RAWS

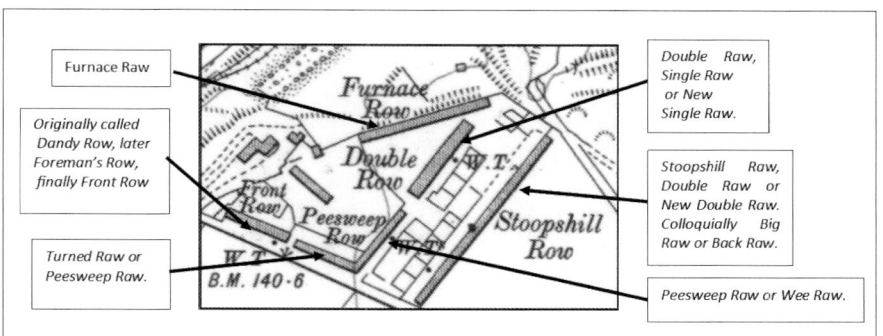

Various names by which raws in Peesweep were known. Detail from OS Map, Ayrshire Sheet XI NE Revised 1909, Published 1911, 6 inches to the mile, reproduced with the permission of The National Library of Scotland.

which led to one of the oral history respondents pointing out that they had three bedrooms. But there was already a raw called Double Row because of its back to back construction. This may have led to confusion and in valuation rolls from 1895 the new raw of rooms and kitchens was called New Double Row and the older back to back raw of single ends was called New Single Row, even though it was 40 years old. In 1951 the valuation rolls reverted to calling it Stoopshill Row. Adding to the variety of names, some oral history interviewees referred to this raw as Back Raw or Big Raw, but I have not found any written records of these names.

To any genealogists trying to identify exactly where in Peesweep their ancestors lived using addresses given on birth, death or marriage certificates, and census returns, consideration must be given to the date of the record as the same address can refer to different raws depending on the year.

One wonders how the postal service managed to deliver letters given this confusion but in those days there would be few letters posted, the postman presumably got to know the current names of the raws and if in doubt could ask clarification of any residents who were around.

My findings are summarised in the map showing the various names by which raws in Peesweep were known.

CARSEHEAD ROWS

Originally there was only one raw called Carsehead Row which was later extended on both ends. This continued to be officially called Carsehead Row, but residents and local people called the first raw after the bridge over the river, 'First Raw'. The middle section which was the oldest was named 'Sticket Raw' and the section furthest from the river was named 'Wee Sticket Raw'. (In the oral histories, the point is made that 'Sticket' can mean failed, unfinished or incomplete and one of the interviewees believed that the name was used because Baird had promised two storeys on the houses

THE DALRY RAWS

but then decided to 'sticket' one.)

When a new raw was built across the road at almost right angles to the existing raws it was officially named Carsehead New Row, but residents and locals called it 'Tarry Raw' or 'Torry Raw', even in some census records because it was roofed with tarred felt. When this New Row was built the original extended raw was officially called Carsehead Old Row. These findings are summarised in labels on the map, 'Various names by which raws in Carsehead were known', shown on the facing page.

Naming of the raws in various official documents	1855 map large scale	1885 Valuation roll	1895 Map large scale	1895 & 1905 Valuation rolls	1913 Housing commission report	1915 & all subsequent Valuation rolls
Number of houses						
9	Not yet built	Together named Carsehead Old Row	Together named Carsehead Old Row	Together named Carsehead Old Row	Wee Stickit Row	Together named Carsehead Old Row
10	Carsehead				Stickit Row	
14	Not yet built				First Row	
36	Not yet built	Carsehead New Row, colloquially called Tarry Raw	Carsehead New Row, colloquially called Tarry Raw	Carsehead New Row, colloquially called Tarry Raw	Not mentioned	Not mentioned Demolished

SUMMARY OF DOCUMENTARY EVIDENCE OF HISTORY OF THE RAWS

In the following section I have discussed historical documents relevant to the raws in chronological order, providing an account of the establishment and development of Carsehead and Peesweep.

THE DALRY RAWS

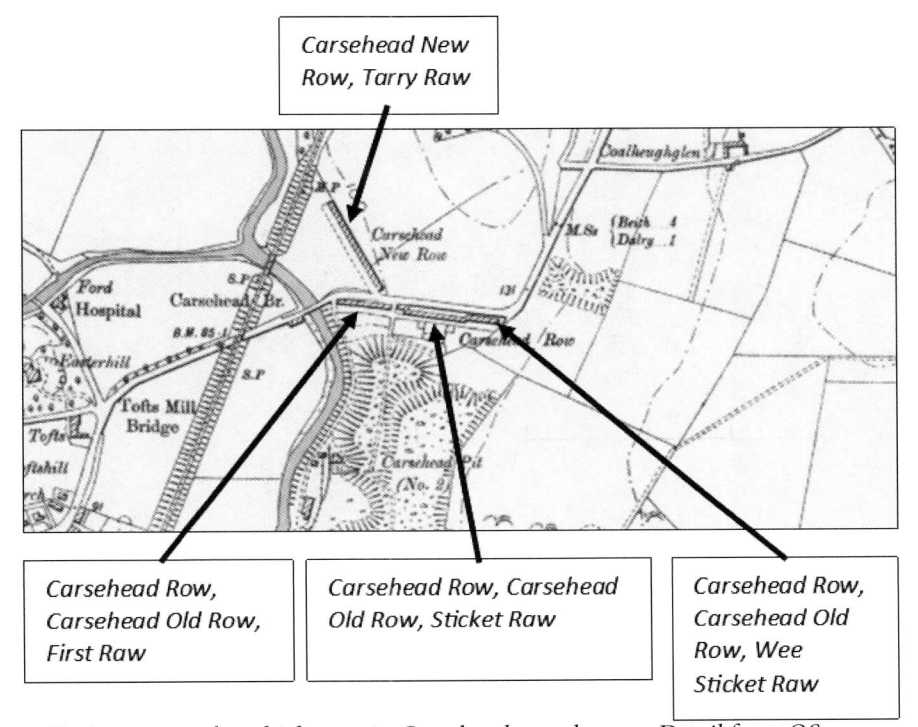

Various names by which raws in Carsehead were known. Detail from OS map. Ayrshire Sheet XI.NE 1895, reproduced with the permission of The National Library of Scotland.

1848 SALE NOTICE FOR IRONWORKS

The full transcription of this document is produced in the section on A Brief History of Mining Coal and Ironstone in Dalry - Ironstone. In it miners' raws are mentioned in this way:

'There are, besides the Manager's House and store buildings, 187 Workmen's houses in a habitable state attached to the Furnaces and Pits and there are 20 partly built which could be finished at a small additional outlay.'

This is the earliest record I have found of the raws. Unfortunately, it does not state where these raws were situated beyond mentioning that they are 'attached to the furnaces and pits'. Neither does this document name them but it seems likely that it refers to Peesweep and Carsehead and perhaps Brick Raw which were nearest to the ironworks.

1851 CENSUS

My great, great, great grandparents, John Creily and Agnes Penman were living in Peesweep Raw. They were the grandparents of Margaret Creily, my great grandmother in the photo entitled, 'My great grandparents and eight of their children'.

THE DALRY RAWS

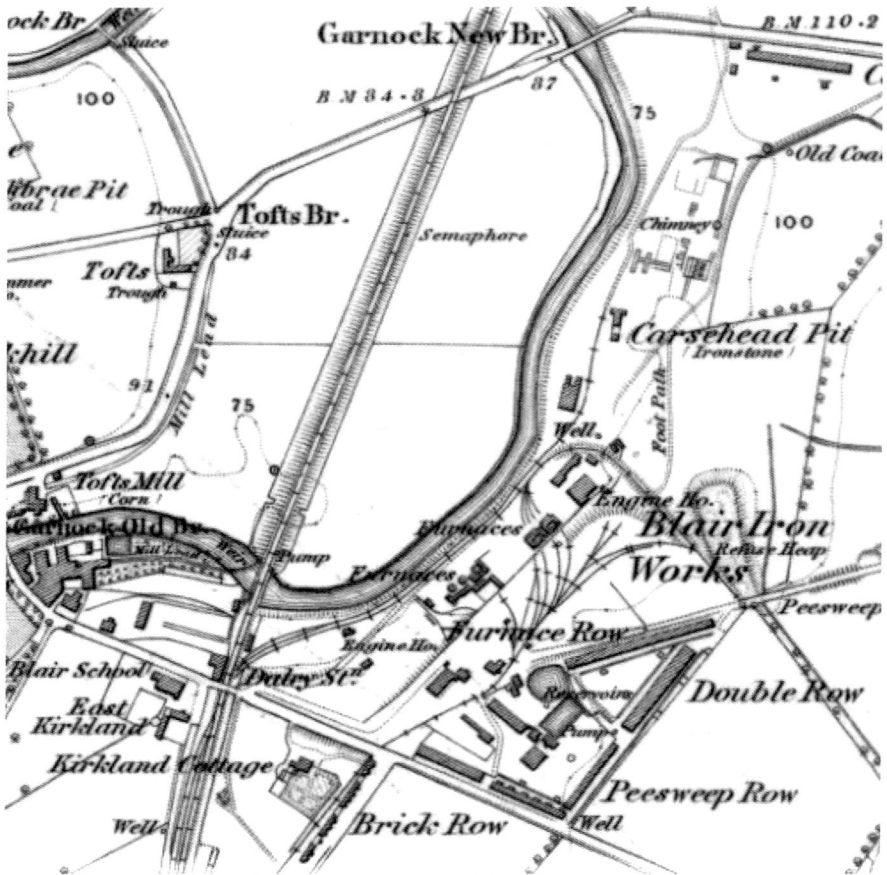

Position of raws and some named. Detail from OS Map, Ayrshire Sheet XI.4 (Dalry) 6 inches to the mile, Survey date 1855, reproduced with the permission of the National Library of Scotland.

In the same census, another great, great, great grandfather, John Greer was living with his son, daughter-in-law and two grandchildren in Dandy Row.

1855 Ordnance Survey Maps

The detail of the 1855 map entitled, 'Position of raws and some named' is the earliest map to name some of the raws. It is also the first record of the position of the ironworks and Blair School.

At Carsehead one raw is seen and labelled 'Carsehead Row'. There are five raws at Peesweep but only three are labelled: 'Furnace Row, Double Row and Peesweep Row'. This and other maps of the same year are the only documentary evidence I have been able to find for the existence of Brick Raw. This map also illustrates how the outlook from both groups of raws was onto industrial installations: Carsehead onto a coal pit and Peesweep

THE DALRY RAWS

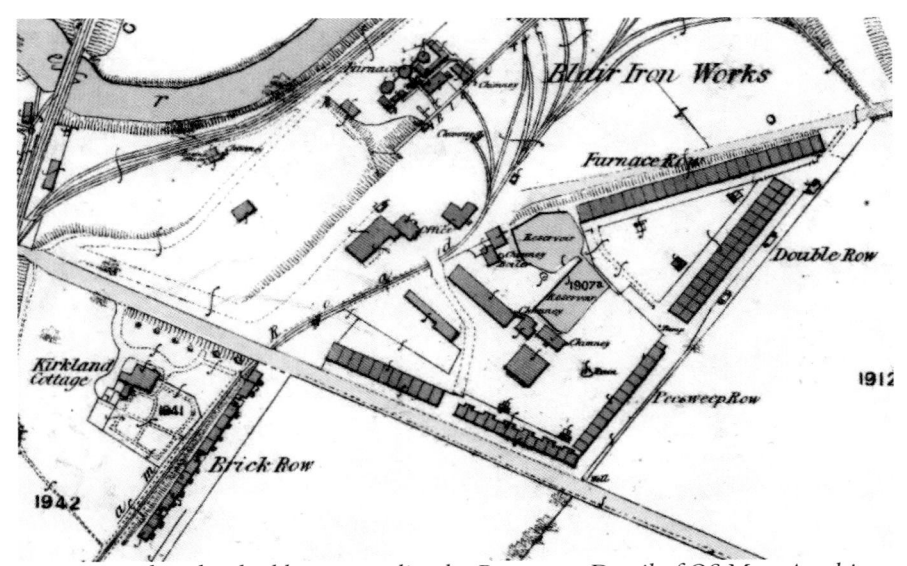

Map – with individual houses outlined – Peesweep. Detail of OS Map, Ayrshire Sheet XI.4 (Dalry) 25 inches to the mile, Survey date 1855, reproduced with the permission of the National Library of Scotland.

onto reservoirs for cooling furnaces. It was common for raws to be in close proximity to such reservoirs and I wonder whether they were fenced off as otherwise they must have been a constant danger to children playing outside the raws. There are also numerous unidentified, presumably industrial buildings which many of the houses overlook.

That same year a map with a greater scale was produced – 25 inches to the mile. A detail is entitled 'Individual houses outlined – Peesweep'. This map allows us to see how many individual houses were in each raw. Also, Double Row/New Single Row can be seen to be built in a back-to-back arrangement. The houses on Blair Road are not named but one raw has small porches facing away from the main road and assuming that the porches are at the front of the houses this must be 'Turned Raw' mentioned in the oral histories. The gap between this raw and the one at right angles to it is clearer because of the larger scale. The map seems to name these two raws at right angles to each other Peesweep Row. There do not appear to be any wash houses or privies. Chimneys for the furnaces are identified and a pump, presumably for drinking water for the residents appeared. Two small buildings are labelled, 'office'. Brick Row is included in maps of this year only, indicating that it was short lived. A siding from the Glasgow railway line runs in front of Brick Row, under Blair Road, passes between the raws and the offices and enters the ironworks. Brick Row and part of the siding were situated where the lane from Blair Road to Finlay Avenue runs today.

THE DALRY RAWS

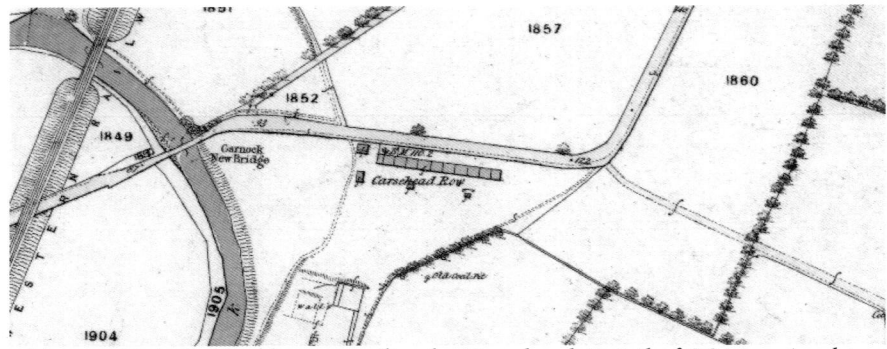

Map – with individual houses outlined – Carsehead. Detail of OS Map, Ayrshire Sheet XI.4 (Dalry) 25 inches to the mile, Survey date 1855, reproduced with the permission of The National Library of Scotland.

Another detail entitled, 'Individual houses outlined – Carsehead' from the same map as before indicates that there were ten houses in the original Carsehead Row with a small building attached to the gable end and two separate buildings. Again there were no wash houses or privies.

1855 Valuation Roll

Neither Carsehead nor Peesweep Raws is explicitly mentioned in the first valuation roll for Dalry parish in 1855 but it mentions colliers' houses which I believe include the Carsehead and Peesweep raws. This can be seen in the table of transcriptions of excerpt from 1855 Valuation Roll:

Description and Situation of Subject	Proprietor	Yearly Rent or Value
Ironworks consisting of 5 blast furnaces with Engines, Machinery and Workshops	Eglinton Iron Company Kilwinning or Blair Iron Company Dalry	£1050
17 ironstone pits with Engines, Fittings and Buildings	ditto	£966
3 coal pits with Engines, Fittings and Buildings	ditto	£97
Sundry Railways	ditto	£157
Colliers' and other houses with store and counting house	ditto	£950
Park at Carsehead	ditto	£14
Kersland Land	ditto	£70

(All transcriptions of valuation rolls, census records and other information extracted from them are courtesy of Scotland's People, National Register of Scotland.)

THE DALRY RAWS

James Baird was involved in both the Eglinton and Blair ironworks as partner in the former and owner of the latter. In cases like this where two companies operated so closely, for business reasons the ownership of assets such as houses were sometimes passed from one company to the other. To complicate things further, Blair owned the land. This explains apparent discrepancies between valuation rolls of different years. At that time, any property with a yearly rent value of less than £4 was not explicitly recorded. Collections of such houses with the same owner were aggregated and the total value recorded.

I believe that the entry under 'Colliers' and other houses with store and counting house' includes Carsehead Raw and Peesweep Raws, and possibly Brick Raw because we know they existed according to the 1855 map, and they are not mentioned more explicitly anywhere else on the valuation roll. Furthermore, entries in the roll are grouped together according to physical proximity. Some nearby raws apart from Peesweep and Carsehead may be included in this entry, for example Kersland, The Den and Patrick's Raw.

A store is mentioned along with the houses and the presence of a company store near miners' raws was common. Although not labelled in any map I have seen, it was presumably housed in one of the un-named buildings. In the oral histories, Wullie Caig says that it overlooked the brickworks but was in ruins by 1940. We do not know if this store was originally run along truck lines as in many mining villages. The truck system at its worst consisted of paying miners in tokens which could only be exchanged in the company store. Goods in the store could be up to 25% more expensive than in other shops, resulting in the miner returning almost all his wages to his employer. There were also practices designed to keep the miner in constant debt.

In 1865 the occupier of the store at Peesweep was the Co-operative Society. This is not the same body as the Scottish Co-operative Wholesale Society which did not come into being until three years later in 1868. A Mr Whitelaw who was a partner in Messrs Baird was interviewed regarding the operation of their stores in Lanarkshire and Ayrshire for the Royal Commission enquiry into the truck system in 1871 (Bowen & Sellar). We can assume that his answers applied to the Dalry store although this was 16 years after its inception and we cannot know how it was operated in the preceding years.

From Mr Whitelaw's answers, it would appear that by 1871 the store was co-operative in the sense that purchasers shared the profits in the form of a 4% to 8% dividend. However it did not adhere to the co-operative principle of management by the members, since the company appointed three of the 15 of the managing committee. These three held the positions of chief cashier and two of the principal managers. The other twelve were selected from workers who had personally lent money to contribute to the capital required to finance the store. They tended to be oversmen or 'men of that stamp' and received 8% interest on their loan.

This discrimination between 'men of that stamp' and other miners hints at disrespect for the men who toiled underground to keep the business profitable and Mr Whitelaw in a job. Furthermore, it appears from Mr Whitelaw's answers that at that time there continued to be a relationship between the miners being paid only a portion of what they had earned (and this in arrears) and their receiving credit in the store so that they were constantly in debt.

According to the valuation rolls the treasurers in Dalry were Thomas Wellwood in 1865, David Pringle (storekeeper) in 1875, Blair Ironworks Co-operative from 1885 to 1915 and from 1925 – 1935 it lay empty. By 1940 it did not exist, presumably lying empty and deteriorating.

The counting house mentioned was the office for administering the business, keeping records, and paying employees. As already mentioned, an 1855 map labels some buildings among the raws, 'office'. If this was the office where employees were paid it seems strange to modern eyes that it should be positioned among the workers' accommodation instead of within the place of work but this highlights how the raws were considered by owners to be part of the industrial plant.

1855 – 1857 Ayrshire Ordnance Survey Name Books, Volume 20
This publication listed and described place names recorded on maps, mentioning Peesweep Row, Furnace Row, Double Row and Carsehead Row. They were all described as 'rows of small dwelling houses occupied by the workmen employed at Blair Iron Works'. All were described as being the property of the company and mention was made of Double Row's back-to-back construction which could be seen on the Ordnance Survey map of the time.

1865 Valuation Roll
The houses at Carsehead Row were named explicitly and although the houses at Peesweep were not named, we can be more confident that the valuation roll referred to them, as can be seen in the table, 'Excerpt from 1865 valuation roll'. Again, individual tenants were not mentioned because the yearly rent was less than £4.

THE DALRY RAWS

Description and Situation of Subject	Proprietor	Feu duties to whom payable	Yearly rent or value
Ironworks consisting of 5 blast furnaces with Engines, Machinery and Connections	Eglinton Iron Company Kilwinning, viz. James Baird, George Baird, Alexander Whitelaw, David Wallace, William Weir, individual partners thereof	Captain WF Blair of Blair	£1200
Houses, store and Counting House at Blair Ironworks and houses at Kersland	ditto		£544
Houses at Carsehead	ditto		£209

1875 VALUATION ROLL

Again, individual tenants of the raws were not named but some individuals who lived in houses valued at more than £4 annual rent were mentioned including their occupation. One miner was named because he occupied a house with annual rent more than £4. The value of some of the individual buildings associated with the ironworks is given. Some houses at Hourat (probably Swinlees) were mentioned but they must have been small in number since they were worth only £8 in annual rent. See the table, 'Excerpt from 1875 valuation roll" on the following page.

THE DALRY RAWS

Description of Subject	Proprietor	Occupier	Yearly Rent or Value
Ironworks	Eglinton Iron Company Kilwinning, viz. James Baird, Alexander Whitelaw, David Wallace, William Weir, individual partners thereof	Selves	£100
Cottage at Blairworks	ditto	James Stevenson Frew, Cashier	£14 10s
Blair Foundry	ditto	Hugh McCully, founder	£40
Counting House	ditto	selves	£12
Store	ditto	David Pringle, Storekeeper	£30
House at Blair	ditto	Selves for tenants under £4	£334 12s
House	ditto	Archibald Cunningham, Underground Manager	£14 10s
ditto	ditto	John Stevenson, weigher, Dalry Iron Company	£5 14s
ditto	ditto	Alexander Dunsmuir, Contractor	£15
ditto	ditto	James Murray, Miner, Dalry	£5 8s
Houses at Stoopshill	ditto	Selves for workmen's houses	£8
Houses at Hourat & Hawkhill	ditto	Selves for workmen's houses	£5
Houses at Carsehead	ditto	Selves for workmen's houses	£180

THE DALRY RAWS

1885 Valuation roll

The Eglinton Iron Company owned all the houses. The Bairds were partners in this company. For the first time, the names and occupations of all householders were recorded, no matter the rental value of the property. Appendix 1 provides a list of the names of all the heads of household resident in Peesweep and Carsehead in 1885.

An additional raw had been built at Peesweep, named Double Row in the early valuation rolls and New Double Row in later rolls. The same raw was entitled Stoopshill Row on maps and in the later Housing Commission report, as described in the earlier section entitled 'Naming the Raws'.

Where before there were only 10 houses in Carsehead Row, this had now been expanded to 32 houses and re-named Carsehead 'Old Row'. As already mentioned, 36 houses had been built across the road in a raw named 'New Row'. These changes are illustrated in the map entitled 'Position of Peesweep and Carsehead Rows'. Locals called New Row 'Tarry Raw' or 'Torry Raw' because the roof was made of tarred felt. This practice was commented on by the Commissioner appointed to inquire into The Mines and Collieries Act 1842 and the state of the population in the mining districts in 1859.

'At their works at Kilsyth, under the Campsie Hills the Messrs Baird have tried the experiment of roofing with prepared cotton-cloth, at one third the cost of ordinary roofing. The material is calculated to last ten years, and is renewable at a cost of 9 pence per yard, with the cost of putting up: an additional room can consequently be given at less cost.'

Despite the 'economy' of roofing the houses with tarred felt, Carsehead New Row had the same number of rooms as Carsehead Old Row, thus belying the implication that savings on roofing would be used to provide extra rooms for the residents.

These observations perhaps explain how, although it was officially New Row, the old raw outlasted it. I very much doubt that Mr Baird or the commissioner of the report lived in a house with a tarry roof.

In the Peesweep raws, James Criely, a miner, probably my great, great grandfather was living in Furnace Row. In the 1881 census he had been living in Wee Peesweep Row but this 'flitting' between houses is not unusual since the residents of Peesweep tended to move house quite frequently.

1895 Map

See the map on page 78, 'Comparing aerial photograph 1944 with map 1895, Peesweep' and 'Comparing aerial photograph 1944 with map 1895, Carsehead.' This map illustrates how the surroundings appear slightly less industrial with the demolition of Blair Ironworks and the removal of the reservoirs. Some land may have been laid out as gardens or drying greens.

THE DALRY RAWS

One of the buildings in the middle of Peesweep area is identified as a smithy.

1895 Valuation Roll

This was the first valuation roll to allocate numbers to individual houses in the raws. Baird and Company owned all the houses from now on. The same raws were named as ten years previously. A few people had started to rent two houses, often, but not always adjacent to each other. Several of my ancestors were resident in Peesweep at that time, namely my great, great uncle James Gallacher at 10 New Single Row; great, great uncle Frank Gallacher at 14 Furnace Row; great, great grandfather James Criely at 16 Furnace Row; and great, great, great uncle John Criely at 10 Double Row.

1905 Valuation Roll

Numbers 11 and 12 Peesweep Raw became the reading room. This appears to have been a community provision and is further discussed in the conclusion. It is first mentioned in the valuation roll of 1905 and last mentioned in that of 1930 but was remembered in the 1950s although reduced to rubble by then. By this time, eight houses were empty in New Single Row and 10 in New Double Row. Four were empty in Carsehead New Row. This could have been a sign of the deterioration of the fabric of the houses.

The 1905 valuation roll for the first time itemises the cost of 'rent, drainage, lighting & scavenging and water'. Scavenging relates to the removal of human sewage from 'dry closets'. A dry closet is a toilet which is not connected to a water supply or sewer. People used a small building to deposit their human waste, either directly or by emptying a pot which had been used in the house. Human sewage and ashes from domestic fires were piled together, hence the frequent interchange between the terms 'dry closet' and 'ash pit'. Sometimes other types of rubbish were also thrown in although most rubbish was burned on the coal fires in the houses. It is concerning to note that between 1895 and 1905 drainage, lighting and scavenging were mentioned in the valuation rolls yet the evidence to the Royal Commission in 1913 described the drainage as inadequate and sewage running in the road to settle outside the doors of the houses. Water, for which residents now paid extra, was provided by shared outside stand-pipes and the reporters stated that provision was inadequate, in some cases consisting of one 'well' shared by two rows.

Local council employees did not perform scavenging or cleansing of ashpits/dry closets, but local farmers paid the council for the right to remove the mixture of sewage and ashes as they used it for fertiliser, as illustrated by the following excerpt from the local newspaper, the *Ardrossan and Saltcoats Herald* 30 November 1906:

THE DALRY RAWS

Dalry Committee on Lighting and Cleansing

'The Dalry Sub Committee on Lighting, Cleansing etc met on Monday evening- Mr Aitken in the chair- when there were also present- Messrs Geddes, Russell, R Gray, RL Riddet, P Muir, T Orr, H Boyd and J Riddet with Mr W Carrick, Clerk.

Cleansing

Offers for the cleaning of ashpits at Blair Works Row were opened. Mr William Kirkpatrick offered £3 to the committee for the refuse, he doing the cleansing; Mr William Ewing offered to do the cleansing for a sum of £4. One of the offerers, pointing out the difficulty of cleansing these ashpits wrote that, 'they had to be put out to be put in.' The offer of £3 was accepted. Mr Gilbert gets the Tarry Row refuse: and Mr Wotherspoon gets the Carsehead Row. Contractors are to be bound to do the work to the satisfaction of the superintendent, failing which the ashpits will be cleared at the expense of the defaulter.'

Kenneth Phillips (one of the oral history interviewees) had a professional connection with the raws when scavenging was current as he worked as a sanitary inspector at that time. He remembers a legal case when the owner (a farmer) of a tenement building near Auchengree around 1946, left it untenanted and therefore thought it was not necessary to empty the midden. However, there was a shortage of housing after the war and squatters moved into the house and used the dry closet and ashpit. This eventually became a problem because no-one emptied it and it overflowed. The farmer did not empty it because he was not receiving rent. It then became a health hazard. The outcome of the legal proceedings was that the owner of the building was eventually held responsible because the law states that if the author of the nuisance cannot be found the owner of the building is responsible. Because they were squatters it was difficult to identify them, but easy to identify the owner of the building.

(Kenneth stated that farmers in later years became reluctant to take human excrement as fertiliser because it contained heavy metals from women's make up.)

Regarding gas street lighting, an article in the *Ardrossan and Saltcoats Herald* of 6 March 1896 reported that the Lighting Committee considered a report as to the recommended position of gas street lamps at Peesweep and Carsehead but when the lamps were installed is not recorded. 'Messrs William Baird & Co did not provide lighting in any of their numerous properties; while the Ayrshire coalmasters stated that 'the lighting of villages was not usual" (according to evidence submitted to the Royal Commission on Housing in Scotland in 1913.) There was a gasworks with two gasometers in Dalry shown in the 1855 map, sited where the public park is now. In later years it was known as the Gas Lighting Company and there was only one gasometer. This would have provided gaslighting inside houses as well as street lighting but when it was provided to the raws is unknown.

1909 Map

Examining the map on page 16, 'Position of Peesweep and Carsehead Raws', it is interesting to note that Carsehead New Row (Tarry Raw) was still standing as it had disappeared four years later when the Housing Commission visited in 1913.

Just off this detail of the map is recorded the Ayr County Council Sewage Tank and I thought that this recorded the installation of flush toilets at Carsehead Raws. However, the later Housing Commission Report makes it clear that there were no flush toilets in 1913. The proximity of sewage provision suggests that it must have been relatively easy and cheap to provide flush toilets and perhaps this is why Carsehead had flush toilets by 1929 but Peesweep never acquired them according to some sources. (Others state that there were flush toilets by the 1940s.)

It has been recognised that miners' raws in the early years were usually built cheek by jowl with heavy industry but this had changed in later years. It is ironic to note that at this time at Carsehead although the towering iron works had by then been removed, it was deemed acceptable to build a killing hoose or slaughterhouse within yards of domestic dwellings.

1911 Census

As already mentioned, my great grandparents, Michael Gallacher and Margaret Criely, were living at 11 New Single Raw with their extended family. I believe that they were perhaps renting two adjacent houses to accommodate everyone as number 12 is not mentioned in the census. This would provide them with two single ends or two rooms for the 14 people itemised in the table, below, excerpted from the 1911 census.

Name	Relationship to head of household	Age	Occupation	In Photo
Michael Gallacher	Head	44	Iron miner (hewer)	√
Margaret Gallacher	Wife	43		√
James Gallacher	Son	19	Iron miner (hewer)	√
John Gallacher	Son	17	Iron miner (hewer)	√

Francis Gallacher (my grandfather)	Son	15	Pony driver (Pit head)	√
Nellie Gallacher	Daughter	13	School	√
Maggie Gallacher	Daughter	11	School	√
Michael Gallacher	Son	9	School	√
Andrew Gallacher	Son	7	School	X -Not yet born
Alexander Gallacher	Son	5	School	X-Not yet born
Susan Gallacher	Daughter	2		X-Not yet born
Francis Gallacher	Brother	37	Iron miner (hewer)	X
Mary Gallacher	Niece	17	Worsted Spinner	X
Nellie Gallacher	Niece	14	Worsted Spinner	X

(Patrick Gallacher who appeared in Photo 1 died in a roof fall in 1910 - one year before the census data were recorded for this table.)

Although overcrowding was almost inevitable with most families living in room and kitchens, the Gallachers' situation was not typical, with 14 people in two one-roomed houses. Taking fourteen census sheets at random and working out occupancy in Peesweep Raws over 50 years the average is 5.4 people per house with either one or two rooms.

Medical Officer for Health Report 1912

In the Ayr County Medical Officer for Health's report for 1912 he noted that in the Northern District of Ayrshire, reportable diseases such as Diphtheria, Scarlet Fever, and Erysipelas (a skin condition) were most prevalent where the population lived in 'miserable mining rows'. Stevenston, Kilbirnie and Dalry were mentioned as places where these diseases were most prevalent. Housing conditions in Stevenston and Dalry were described as especially bad and responsible for 60% of the Diphtheria cases for all 12 parishes of North Ayrshire.

THE DALRY RAWS

1913 Royal Commission on Housing

This important document has already been mentioned in the General History of Miners' Raws. Reporters to the commission visited Peesweep and Carsehead and criticised them in much the same terms they had used in decrying raws in other parts of Ayrshire. Residents of the raws in later times might be shocked to read how poor the living conditions and upkeep were in 1913. From the contributions to the oral histories in the next section, it is obvious that amenities were greatly improved between 1913 and when respondents were living in the raws. Perhaps these improvements were made partly in response to the evidence summarised in the table, 'Summary of findings of 1913 Royal Commission on Housing on visiting Peesweep and Carsehead', shown here:

Name of raw (& number of houses)	Number of rooms	Number of dry closet / ash pits	Number of wash houses	Number of coal houses	Other comments	Annual Rent
Front Row (11)	2	4	4	none	Coal stored below the bed	£3 12s
Turned Row (12)	1	4/2	none	none	Small porch at doors, dry closets very close to doors	£3 5s
Wee Row (10)	1	2/1	Not mentioned	Not mentioned	Floors 18 inches below surface of the road with consequent dampness and occasional flooding	£3 5s
Furnace Row (23)	2	4/2	None	None	Floor below beds bare earth, coal kept below the bed, dry closets, and ash pits very near doors, provision of water inadequate	£3 12s

Double Row (32)	1	6/3	None	None	Coal kept below the bed, floors uneven and cracked, only 1 water tap for the whole row	Not stated
Stoophill Row (sic) (24)	2 + 2 small cupboard-sized, room for a bed	8/4	None	None	Several houses had to be closed due to subsidence, dry closets, and ash pits very near front doors and sewage flowing from them and settling in front of the houses	£3 18s
Carsehead First Row (14)	2 + 1 cupboard-sized room with bed	6 dry closets without doors	None	None	Tenants have built coal houses and wash houses for themselves, roadway unpaved and very dirty	£3 18s
Stickit Row (10)	2	4 dry closets without doors	None	None	Tenants have built coal houses and wash houses for themselves, Tenants complained they were troubled with rats and dampness	£3 6s

THE DALRY RAWS

| Wee Stickit Row (9) | 2 | 2 without doors/ 1 | None | None | Tenants have built coal houses and wash houses for themselves, | £3 6s |

To put the annual rents in context, the average wage of an underground miner in 1913 was 6 shillings a day. It is unclear whether this is before or after deductions but probably means that rent accounted for a low percentage of the annual outgoing.

1915 Valuation Roll

This of course was during the First World War when the government had to balance the need for miners to continue producing coal; not only for heating and cooking in civilian homes, and provision of power for industry, but also to fuel naval vessels. Ironstone miners were required to supply ironworks with ore to produce armaments. Yet more and more men were required to fight on the front line. Many miners volunteered and 40% of military age had joined up by 1915. Others were enlisted, including my grandfather, Francis Gallacher, and great uncle John Gallacher. Twenty thousand miners were enlisted specifically to use their experience and skills working underground to burrow under enemy trenches and attack from behind. This left a shortage of manpower and consequently of coal throughout the war.

Meantime, nearer home, New Single Row had three empty houses which were described as 'empty (uninhabitable)'.

Ten houses of Peesweep Row were no longer in existence as the part at right angles to Blair Road which locals called 'Wee Raw' had been demolished. Peesweep Row now consisted of the reading room and the 12 houses of Turned Row. At Carsehead, New Row (or 'Tarry Raw') had been demolished but Old Carsehead Row incorporating First Raw and Wee Stickit Raw with its slate roofs continued to house 33 families with only one house lying empty.

New Double Row / Stoopshill Row had reduced from 34 houses to 22 due to demolition of eight houses, presumably those described as subject to subsidence in the 1913 Housing Commission report.

1920s-Building of First Council Houses

The 1920s saw the start of local councils taking responsibility for housing working class families and the start of people leaving the raws for the first council houses in Dalry in Townend Street, Garnock Street, Lynn Avenue and Merksworth Avenue. They were known locally as the 'Wheatley

THE DALRY RAWS

Houses', as already mentioned.

Between 1919 and 1948, 25,000 new houses were built in Ayrshire. Many people moved from the raws directly to council houses. In Dalry, as in many other towns, the two main surges in council house building were in the late 1920s and the mid-1950s. Members of my family benefitted from these periods of intense council house building. My great, great grandparents, Michael Gallacher and Margaret Criely, first moved from Peesweep to another private let in Vennel Street where Margaret died. Michael, their daughters Margaret and Susan and his brother Francis later moved to a council house in Merksworth Avenue.

1925 VALUATION ROLL
There appears to have been some stabilisation of the condition of the houses which did not change between 1915 and 1925.

1930 VALUATION ROLL
Most of the remaining raws were owned by William Baird and Company except for New Double Row which was owned by Blair Trust Company. A few houses were uninhabitable including one at the end of the remaining houses in New Double Row. The store still lay empty. The following surnames of heads of households in this valuation roll may belong to the parents of some of the contributors to the Oral Histories: Kirk, Cairns, Harkins, Morrison, Simpson, Ward.

A James Gallacher was there and he might have been my great uncle, from the family photograph.

1935 VALUATION ROLL
New Double Raw had reduced by another four houses, leaving only 18 where there had originally been 34. It is ironic that so much of the most recently built raw had to be abandoned in a similar way in which New (Tarry) Row at Carsehead was short lived. The deterioration of these relatively new houses may have been due to poor construction or poor choice of site or a combination of the two. As early as 1913 the housing commission had reported that houses in New Double Row / Stoopshill Row were subject to subsidence. The reading room was not mentioned in 1935, presumably demolished.

1940S
In an aerial photograph of Peesweep in 1944, faint outlines of the houses which had been demolished in Wee Row and New Double Row/Stoopshill Row can be seen. Furnace Row and Double Row/New Single Row appear to remain the same size, as can be seen in the map, 'Comparing aerial photograph 1944 with map 1895, Peesweep'.

THE DALRY RAWS

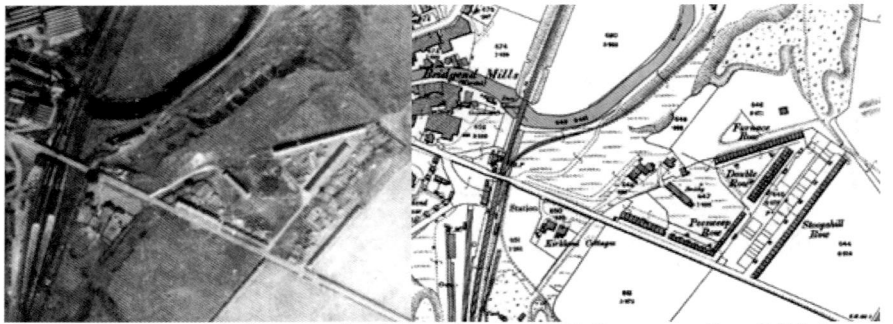

Comparing aerial photograph 1944 with map 1895, Peesweep. Detail OS Air Photo Mosaics of Scotland, 1944-1950, detail, OS Map, Ayrshire sheet XI NE Revised 1895, Published 1897, 6 inches to the mile, reproduced with the permission of the National Library of Scotland.

    At Carsehead, New Row or Tarry Raw had been demolished around 1910. See 'Comparing aerial photograph 1944 with map 1895, Carsehead', where the photograph cuts off part of the 'old' raw but 'new' raw has clearly been demolished, although you can see a faint outline where it used to be.

    I find these aerial photographs somewhat ghostly. There is a shortage of photographs of the raws taken at ground level so it is tantalising to see grainy photographs from the air. We also know that the raws were coming to the end of their existence by 1944. Reading the oral histories, the fondness all the contributors had for the raws comes over clearly and this adds to the atmosphere of nostalgia and sadness for times gone emanating from these photographs. I like to think that people living in the raws on

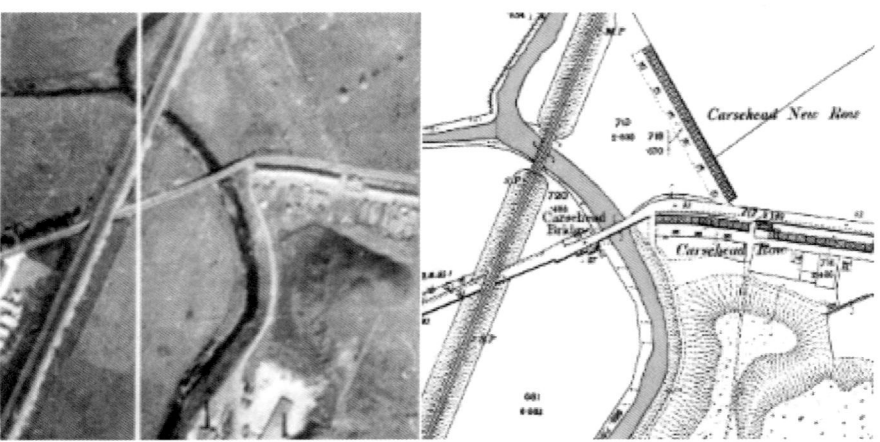

Comparing aerial photograph 1944 with map 1895, Carsehead. Detail from OS Air Photo Mosaics of Scotland, 1944-1950, and detail, OS Map, Ayrshire Sheet XI NE Revised 1895, Published 1897, 6 inches to the mile, reproduced with the permission of the National Library of Scotland.

THE DALRY RAWS

that day heard the aeroplane overhead and looked up from fetching water, blethering with neighbours, hanging out washing, tending their gardens or playing outside.

Oblique aerial photograph of Dalry, 1946. Photo copyright Historic Environment Scotland, license for use granted.

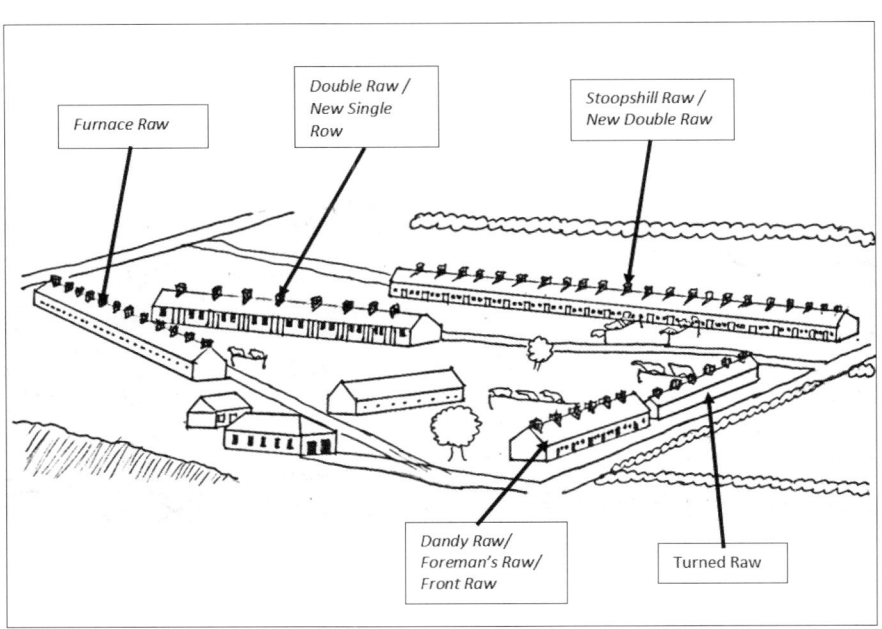

Sketch of Peesweep Rows Taken from oblique aerial photograph, 1946. (Eighteen houses from New Double Row/ Stoopshill Row and twelve from Wee Row had been demolished by 1946 and several houses in other rows, though still standing, were deemed uninhabitable.)

THE DALRY RAWS

Two years later an aeroplane again flew above Dalry and took a photo on a clear sunny day. Peesweep raws can be discerned at the top right and Carsehead raws at the top left. See 'Oblique aerial photograph 1946'. This time the photograph was taken at an oblique angle from a lower height but the raws are too far away to allow a clear view.

The oblique aerial photo shows the raws only in the distance and zooming into the Peesweep area on the larger photograph made it too unclear to reproduce. However I was able to make a sketch from the photo which illustrates the lay out of the raws. See the sketch of Peesweep Rows from oblique aerial photograph, 1946.

Looking back from 1940 to the first valuation roll to name the heads of household much had changed in the raws, including the prevalence of mining as the occupation of the head of the household as illustrated in the following table, Comparing occupations 1885 and 1940, Peesweep and Carsehead combined:

Year	No. of houses	Miners as head of household	Widows as head of household	Labourers as head of household	Other occupations as head of household	% miners
1885	170	155	6	5	Bricklayer Carter Railway signalman Iron Foundry	94.5%
1940	119	53	17	32	Millworker x3 Railwayman Brickworker x2 Weaver Dynamite Worker Steelworker None stated x7	44%

As well as illustrating the change in occupation of the heads of household this table records the reduction of houses in Peesweep and Carsehead from 170 to 119 due to demolition often caused by subsidence. It is hardly surprising that they were prone to subsidence since the land they stood on was literally undermined!

Although in 1885 the figure for miners as heads of households was high at 94.5% it could be that the men with other occupations nevertheless worked in the mines, making it possible that 100% of the household heads worked for the same company. In this way the raws were tied houses, only available to employees of owners. This situation had changed by 1940 with the decline in mining in the area. The number of heads of households who were miners had reduced to 44%. By 1948 it had further reduced to 32%. It could be that over time as fewer houses were required for miners, the owners rented more and more to people outwith their employ. This would of course provide income to the owners but in a period of housing shortage these houses are likely to have been in high demand by manual workers in other industries.

The increase in the number of widows is striking and may be due to the war or an ageing population as young families were allocated council houses and moved away from the raws.

The table also shows a large increase in the number of heads of households who described themselves as labourers. I presume many of them worked in brickworks which were replacing mines as the main industry. I find it interesting that miners never describe themselves as labourers although their work must surely be a type of manual labour. This is probably due to the strong culture within the mining occupation which encouraged pride in being a miner, solidarity with others in the trade and a tradition whereby miners saw themselves as artisans.

1949 – 1955 Valuation Rolls
This period marks the end of Peesweep Rows during which everyone moved out of the raws and the buildings themselves were demolished. Most of the raws were nearly 100 years old by then and had been constructed to low building standards. Although many of the occupants had improved the houses as much as they could, they still did not meet current health requirements. Overcrowding and lack of sanitary provision resulted in their being judged as unfit for human habitation. In Carsehead a large number of residents moved out to new council houses but the buildings were not demolished and they remained under the same ownership by William P. Friels. They continued to be occupied after this period. The following section therefore relates more to Peesweep Rows.

The rolls indicate the following information although it is impossible to be completely accurate with the dates since the year of each valuation roll runs over the end of one and the start of the next calendar year.

1949-50 was the last year before commencement of building post war council housing in Dalry. This was therefore the final year before residents of the raws started to move out in large numbers. Appendix 2 lists the names of heads of households in Peesweep raws and Carsehead recorded in a valuation roll in the late 1940s. The raws at Peesweep were still owned by Baird at this time, except for New Double Row / Stoopshill Row which was owned by the Blair Trust.

In 1950-51 Ayr County Council built the 'Agricultural' houses at the start of Blair Road on the opposite side from the raws. The Scottish Special Housing Association commenced building at West Kilbride Road. This organisation was an administrative body receiving support from the Scottish Office, financed by the UK government. Its aim was to provide social housing where local councils could not do so and also to provide employment. They had areas of particular responsibility such as providing housing in remote areas, for workers required by expanding industrial sites, to relieve overcrowding, and to provide alternative housing for people living in substandard accommodation. The organisation recognised miners as being a discrete group requiring improved housing conditions.

The SSHA started to build Craig Avenue, Crichton Avenue, Kirkland Crescent and Wingfaulds Avenue that year. The first people from the raws to be allocated these new houses started to move out. They were the first people in an exodus lasting five years at the end of which the Peesweep raws would no longer exist. Some of the oral history respondents mention moving from the raws to these streets – the start of the West Kilbride/'Timber' scheme.

In 1951-52 ownership of the raws passed from Baird to Thomas S. Allison, except for New Double Row / Stoopshill Row which continued to be owned by the Blair Trust. Ayr County Council commenced building council houses on the right hand side of Blair Road, the even numbered houses in Douglas Avenue, and the odd numbered houses in Finlay Avenue.

In 1952-53 Ayr County Council continued building on the right hand side of Blair Road with Baidland Avenue and Cleeves Avenue. They commenced building beyond the raws but on the same side in Kerse Avenue and Stoopshill Crescent. Allison and Blair still owned the Peesweep raws but fewer and fewer were occupied as they were deemed uninhabitable. Despite people continuing to move out of the raws when they were allocated council houses, the numbers did not decrease as much as might be expected because such was the demand for houses, people were willing to move into the raws when they were vacated in this way. It is possible to see the names of heads of households in houses in the raws in the valuation roll one year and the same people recorded as the first tenants in the new council houses the following year.

By 1953 - 54 Ayr County Council must have bought out Allison and Blair Trust since the council now owned Foreman's Row, what was left of Peesweep Row, and Stoopshill Row. New Single Row and Furnace Row do not appear in the valuation roll, presumably because they had been demolished. The street of new houses in Stoopshill Crescent was extended.

In 1954-55 the council built Blairlands Drive and continued to own Peesweep Row and Stoopshill Row with only 22 tenants still living in the two remaining raws. Foreman's Row must have been demolished by then since it is not mentioned in the valuation roll.

THE DALRY RAWS

1955–1956 was the last year when any of the raws were occupied. The same 22 heads of households who had been there the previous year moved out at some time this year, Peesweep and Stoopshill rows were demolished, Mair Avenue was built, and the era of miners' raws in Dalry came to an end. The last heads of households resident in the raws were:

PEESWEEP
James McAttee
Helen Nelson
John Gordon
Charles Andrews
Jeanne McGougan
Elizabeth Clark
Joseph King
James Andrews
Edward Magilton
Robert Andrews

STOOPSHILL
Alistair McPherson
Alexander Carswell
Jeanie Sanders
John Fleck
Elizabeth Caig
Thomas McCrae
John Sanders
Catherine McCann
Robert Kirk
Elizabeth Blackwood
Jeanie Davidson
Joseph King

Ayr County Council started building the Lynn scheme this year.
In 1956 -1957 most of the Lynn scheme had been completed and occupied including most of Burnhouse Avenue, Peden Avenue, St Margaret's Avenue, Shaw Place and Wingate Avenue. No-one was living in the Peesweep raws but the valuation roll for Peesweep Row and Stoopshill Row records under tenant/occupier 'sites vacant' and the proprietor is Ayr County Council. Shortly after this Peesweep Row and Stoopshill Row were demolished and built over with the completion of Blair Road and Blairlands Drive.
It should be remembered that the local council placed closing orders on the houses during this period, compelling residents to move whether

they wanted to or not. There were mixed feelings among the residents about leaving the raws with some looking forward to more space and privacy, and plumbing and electricity in a new council house while others were reluctant to leave the close community they had known for so long. No doubt many had mixed feelings. There was often a worry about the cost of council house rents and this is mentioned by some of the respondents in the oral histories.

As already mentioned, the residents of the raws were not the only people living in substandard housing in Dalry at this time. Many families were living in single ends in tenements or subdivided houses and they benefitted from council housing building programmes. In my own family, my maternal grandparents moved from a subdivided house in Vennel Street in 1935 with an annual rateable value of £5 5s to a Wheatley house in Garnock Street by 1940 with a rateable value of £14 10s. But the substandard housing continued to be needed and my parents lived in a single end in a tenement with outside toilet and wash house in Smith Street when they were married at first. When she was expecting her first baby in 1949 my mother did not want to give birth to my older sister in the single end because of the inadequate amenities. She arranged to move back to my grandparents' council house temporarily in order to give birth in a modern, hygienic house with private indoor facilities. They returned to the single end after the birth and my sister was brought up in the single end in Smith Street until 1955 when the family was allocated a brand new council house in Peden Avenue in the Lynn scheme just in time for me to be born there two months later.

It is to be presumed that the majority of families managed to budget for the increased cost although one of the oral history respondents did mention people being evicted from their council house for rent arrears. But think of what people gained for paying their council house rent – a flat or house which was fully plumbed, connected to the sewage system, fully wired electrically, with hall, living room, kitchen, bathroom with WC, two/three bedrooms and a good-sized garden, not to mention that all facilities were fully private. The council house amenities were worth much more than those of a house in the raws, tenements or sub divided houses.

Late 1950s

By this time, 46,000 council houses had been built in Ayrshire and a share of these was built in Dalry as already described. The position of the Wheatley houses and the three 1950s schemes can be seen in the map showing the position of Dalry council housing schemes.

The Peesweep raws and the Blair housing scheme which replaced it can be compared in the map comparing Peesweep raws with Blair Housing Scheme today.

THE DALRY RAWS

Position of Dalry council housing schemes. Detail of Microsoft Bing map, Microsoft product screen shot reprinted with permission from Microsoft Corporation.

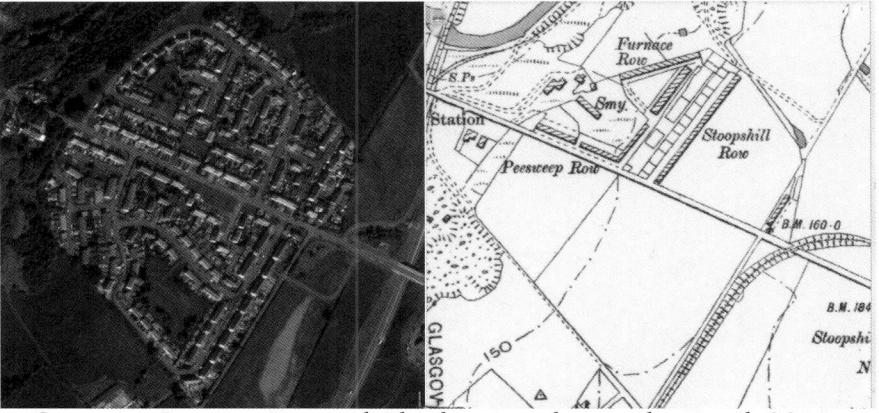

Comparing Peesweep Raws with Blair housing scheme today. Detail, OS Map Ayrshire Sheet XI NE Revised 1895, Published 1897, 25 inches to the mile, reproduced with the permission of The National Library of Scotland, and current Microsoft Bing satellite map. Microsoft product screen shot(s) reprinted with permission from Microsoft Corporation.

The map, 'Overlapping 1895 map with modern satellite map of 'The Blair Scheme' ' makes clear how the Peesweep took up a little more than a quarter of the area now occupied by today's housing, yet at the maximum consisted of 120 houses housing about 650 people.

85

THE DALRY RAWS

Overlapping 1895 map with modern satellite map of "The Blair Scheme". 1892 map of Peesweep Rows overlaid on modern Microsoft Bing satellite image of the area today, reproduced with the permission of the National Library of Scotland. Microsoft product screen shot(s) reprinted with permission from Microsoft Corporation.

Blair Road today. Current photo of houses on Blair Road today where Front Raw and Turned Raw originally stood. There are 16 modern 2 storey houses in the space previously occupied by 23 houses in the two raws.

86

THE DALRY RAWS

The 1950s council-built houses on the left hand side of Blair Road as seen in the photo, 'Blair Road today' replaced Front Row and Turned Row.

The recurring theme of this introduction has been the inadequacy of the miners' raws as dwelling places and the low standard of living they provided. They stood for just over 100 years and appeared to have minimal upgrades in that time, despite official reports recommending thorough improvements or demolition. Landowners and mine owners appear to have ignored these reports or made only minimal upgrades, leaving tenants to live in overcrowded, insanitary conditions. They had no compunction in expecting tenants to live in conditions they would not have tolerated themselves. It was only when a (minority) Labour Government came to power in 1924 that national and local government acted to start to improve the living conditions of the working class.

If we contrast the lifestyles of the residents of the miners' raws and that of the owners and landowners the disparity calls to mind the view of the former Greek Finance Minister, Yanis Varoufakis, when he stated that, 'Capitalism's crisis is that it only encourages misanthropy'.

Oral Histories

This section of the book comprises the oral histories of people who knew either Peesweep or Carsehead. They experienced life in the raws either as residents or visitors and so they are links from the past to the present. I am extremely grateful to all of them for taking the time to talk to me about their memories of the raws. Their stories bring to life the raws in a way that no amount of researching documents ever could.

Methodology for Oral Histories
I tried various methods of contacting people and found that the most effective was to attend social events for retired people in Dalry community venues. Combined with word of mouth ('Snowball Sampling') I identified ten people who had lived in the raws and another three who had direct knowledge of them as frequent visitors. Nine remembered the Peesweep Raws and four remembered Carsehead. Two of the interviewees contacted me in response to an appeal on Facebook for people who remembered the raws.

    I interviewed and audio recorded the oral histories of twelve people who had lived in the raws or been regular visitors to them. A thirteenth completed an informal questionnaire with her son because the family felt that she was not well enough to have a visit from me. These are over and above the two miners' interviews covered earlier.

    The interviews were loosely structured with questions about the physical characteristics of the raws; external and internal appearance; size of rooms; amenities such as lighting and cooking arrangements; level of comfort; hygiene etc. The interviewees also provided information on much wider aspects of life in the raws and Dalry as a whole than I had at first anticipated. I believe this additional information is valuable and I have incorporated it into the final document.

    I listened several times to the audio recordings and summarised as much of the information provided by the interviewees as possible. I tried to represent their stories accurately by only removing repetitions and re-organising information while always aiming to accurately reflect what had been said.

    The interviewees used Scots words to varying degrees, and I have sought to respect this by reproducing verbatim all reported dialogue quoted in speech marks and by using a smattering of Scots words if used by particular interviewees. In this way I hope I have retained the flavour of the language spoken.

THE DALRY RAWS

I also noticed that many of the respondents used the second person when describing life in the Raws; 'You had to clear out when your mother baked'; 'You had a bath in the bine'. I have sometimes retained this form of language, again to reflect the flavour of how the interviewees expressed themselves.

I have occasionally inserted an explanation in my own words of terms used by the interviewees. These appear in square brackets.

Wullie Caig

Wullie was born in 18 New Single Row in 1940. His father's name was also Wullie Caig and his mother was Jessie McEwan. He had an older brother and a younger sister. Wullie explained that New Single Row was built back-to-back. They were single ends. There were 20 houses in total - even numbers on one side and odd numbers on the other. He could chap through the back wall and the neighbours would hear him. Neighbour family names he remembers include Low, Lyndsay, Long and Morrison.

One of the Morrison girls was a successful competitive Highland Dancer and regularly competed in the annual Cowal Games at Dunoon. Wullie remembers her setting off in her 'full regalia'. Stoopshill Raw was also called Big Raw and Stoopshill bing was at the back. The roof spaces in Stoopshill Raw were not separated and it was possible for the residents to travel the length of the whole raw from one end to the other in the roof.

He remembers two men in particular from Turned Raw who kept pigeons: Ward and Houston.

His raw was built on a slope and the lower houses had steps up to the front door because the level of the ground was lower. The houses higher on the hill did not need steps. Sometimes there was a communal step leading to neighbouring front doors. There were slates on the roof. In his family's single end there were two set in beds, a fireplace, two easy chairs, a table with small chairs round it where they ate and a cupboard where the gas

Wullie Caig

masks were kept. There wasn't room for anything else. Coats were hung up on the back of the door and if a neighbour gave them poached rabbits, they were hidden under these coats. All the residents used this arrangement to hide poached rabbits.

His grandparents, an aunt and his father's cousin and family all lived in the raws. His grandfather, Hughie Caig was born in the 1890s and became a professional footballer. He was one of the first Scottish players to play for an English team, Middlesbrough. As such he was more comfortably off and could afford to stay in Front Raw also called Dandy Raw because they were bigger and better houses. After his football career was over he worked as a miner then at the railbank in Glengarnock steelworks. The really well-off people lived in Hillside Cottages which they also called the stables. His friend, Bertie Harkins lived there. His father's cousin, Dick Caig lived in Stoopshill Raw with Wullie's second cousin, Gordon Caig, who is mentioned in other oral histories. [Dick Caig was later my next door neighbour.]

Wullie's great grandfather had a very big picture of King Billy [William of Orange] on his horse up on the wall in his house in Front Raw. Although there were friendships between Protestants and Catholics some adults told them not to associate with Catholics.

There were two wash houses for twenty houses. Each family was allocated one morning or one afternoon. If it rained when it was your turn – 'tough'. People would go round and ask other neighbours if they were using their slot that day as they wanted or needed more time for washing. Wullie said that for his granny, washing was the main event of the week. His mother worked in Fleming and Reid's Mill and did not appear to put as much importance on washing. She probably put the responsibility for their washing onto his granny. Wullie remembers one day when an employee from the water board arrived and required to turn off the water supply while he did some maintenance work. The workman shouted that the water was about to be turned off and all the women came running out to the pumps with various utensils such as pots and kettles to store water until it was turned on again. Wullie remembers this as causing a great commotion and joked that the women might have knocked weans out of the way in their panic to store water. The pump at Front Raw had a nice structure and had a cup attached by a chain but the others were very plain standpipes.

Another workman who was a regular at the raws was Johnnie the lamp man who lit the gas street lights at dusk and turned them off at dawn. Wullie remembers that there were numerous streetlights dotted about between the raws.

There were eight flush toilets for 20 families. You knocked on the doors until you found one which was empty. There was a key but most of the locks were broken. However, they were quite well kept. Newspaper was used as toilet paper and people were often heard shouting for someone to bring them some newspaper because there was none left in the toilet.

When Wullie was two years old he had scarlet fever and was a patient in Irvine Central Hospital. This was during the war and he remembers an air raid siren going off and nurses rushing to shut the curtains. While in hospital he tasted condensed milk and banana for the first time. These were not readily available because of war time rationing.

Once recovered and a little older, he remembers playing outside when German bombers flew over. His grandfather came out and took him indoors. Other war memories include seeing barrage balloons at Stevenston, protecting nearby ICI.

During the war Wullie's father, who had been born in Dalry, worked at ICI in Girvan. Because this related to munitions, he was not called up to the armed forces until 1942. He stayed in Girvan most of the time until then and Wullie does not remember his father being at home much when he was very young. In fact, one time his father and uncle were walking down the street and Wullie shouted 'Hello' from across the road to his uncle but did not greet his father who was taken aback by this. After the war his father was a builder at the Timber scheme and when that job finished, he was a plate layer on the railways at Glengarnock steelworks.

When he was a little older Wullie played at football outside the raws especially at an area they called the 'brickyaird'. This was between Front Raw, Turned Raw and New Single Raw and was outside a building they called 'Rabbie Aird's auld hoose'. Rabbie Aird was the factor for Miss Blair who owned the raws and the building was used to store materials such as bricks and wood for repair and upkeep of the raws. Rabbie Aird was also the rent man, collecting rents for the owners. Next to this was a ruined building which had been the store. It overlooked the brickwork. There was an area of ground nearer New Single Row which was very damp and boggy and was called the 'marsh'. Rushes grew there and it was smelly, with a lot of frogs. You needed wellington boots to walk on it. I showed Wullie old maps with the reservoir marked and he confirmed that the marsh was in the same area. He said that boys and girls played together.

He used to go to the berry picking at the Blair Estate. It was a big annual event with around twenty people employed. You picked blackcurrants, or if you were favoured, strawberries. Mr Howie the gardener weighed the berries you had picked, noted the poundage and you were paid a small amount at the end of the week.

He remembers the joint outings to the shore at Ardneil Bay and to Rouken Glen Park in Glasgow on a Paterson bus. (The local bus company.)

The family left the raws in 1950 and moved into 18 Kirkland Crescent. They were entitled to a council house because there were two adults and three children living in a single end in New Single Raw. They were one of the last families to move into the Timber scheme and after that people moved into the Blair scheme. His father had worked at building the Timber scheme and he said that they were held together with 6-inch nails. [This was a sarcastic comment about the low standard of building work.] After they moved in, there was a fatal housefire in their street which alarmed all the neighbours. They were particularly worried because the houses were timber-clad and they were concerned that this made them more flammable. Residents believed that it may have been caused by a fuse in the electricity meter box igniting a slight gas leak in the gas meter which was housed in the same area. For this reason, Wullie's family and many others switched off the electricity before going to bed at night although the council did alter the position of the meters in all the houses. Wullie also remembers the housefire at Dick Prasher's house nearby. [Also mentioned by Kenny Phillips.]

Wullie Caig's grandmother and brother behind Front Raw with Turned Raw in the background, photo courtesy of Wullie Caig, enhanced by Hugh Anderson.

Wullie remembers the houses in the Blair Scheme being built. The area between Cleeves Avenue, the top end of Baidland Avenue and Douglas Avenue was used by the workmen for storage of materials and a base for the men. It later became an informal football pitch which they called the 'Jiners' Park' [joiners' park]. [This area is still grassed and my sons played football there in the 1990s.] Although he lived in Kirkland Crescent in the timber scheme by then, he went to his granny's house in Cleeves Avenue after school, so he was able to play football at the Jiners' Park with Brian McNicol, Ian McKenzie, Joe Houston, Cliff Long, Paddy McGuigan, and Jim McKerral. There was a tendency for the raws people to continue to associate with previous neighbours even after the raws had been demolished and they had moved into council houses.

THE DALRY RAWS

When Wullie was at Dalry High, the rector was Mr Holland who had the nickname, 'Dutchy'. He was a nice man and lived at Strands, Braehead, next door to Andy Glen who was the owner of the Roxy Picture House in Garnock Street. When Wullie left school his first job was in the traffic office in Glengarnock Steelworks. He was there from 1955 and developed a career in steel manufacturing until it closed in 1987 then he worked in the headquarters of A T Mays, travel agents in Saltcoats. He met his wife, Iris at Glengarnock Steelworks and they had a daughter and two sons. He is widowed now and still lives in Dalry. He provided the photo, ' Wullie Caig's grandmother and brother'.

Ella Burns Cairns

Ella was born at 30 Carsehead Row in 1932. She had five sisters and two brothers. Her Granny was at number 7 Sticket Row, in the oldest building. Ella left when she was 18 in 1950 to move into 4 Kirkland Crescent. Her father had worked in the steelworks before the war, served in the army during the First World War, then worked in Finlay brickworks. There were ten people in three rooms. The six girls all slept in the same room, their parents slept in the living room and two brothers slept in a wee room at the back with a 'set-in bed'. [This was a bed whose frame was built into the fabric of the building in an alcove, usually off a public room. They are also sometimes called bed recesses, recessed beds, or box beds.] Ella remembers that there was no running water in the house. You had to carry water from the wash house into the house. There were flush toilets at the side of the wash houses. Two families shared each toilet and there were four toilets to each wash house. This means that there was one wash house to eight families. There was a scullery where you kept fresh water. When children were too big to be bathed in the house, they went for a bath in the wash house.

Ella had an aunt living at nearby Little Acre rows and they had dry toilets. They cooked on a range and also had a gas ring. There was gas lighting. The scullery was used if Ella's mother was baking, and everyone had to clear out because baking was a big upheaval and there were so many people and not much room.

Outside there were lovely

Ella Burns Cairns

big gardens across from the houses but not attached to them and men grew vegetables there. The ground between the garden and the house was trampled earth and you took your shoes off when you went inside to prevent trailing in the dirt. There were uncovered sinks outside to empty dirty water. Most waste was burned but what could not be burned was put in bins for collection. Inside there was linoleum and carpet (not fitted), a sideboard, big chairs but no settee, and a table. There was not a lot of room. In the scullery was kept a pail of cold water, a wee pail for rubbish and a bucket of coal. (There were coal houses outside and the coal man came round with a horse and cart.) There was also a wardrobe and chest of drawers, as well as the set-in bed.

As a child Ella remembers playing in the wee burn and playing hide and seek in a drain. She looks back on this with amusement now. She had a doll's pram which had been handed down from an older child and later she had a bike. She played at shops and liked to get water and pretend to make butter out of mud. In the summer when it was really hot, tar bubbled in the streets and if you got it on your socks it was impossible to get off. In winter when it snowed they sledged down the bing on their mothers' trays. The bing was a large heap of waste from the nearby mines. When Wullie Hamilton came round with his hardware van her mother had to buy new trays. There was a golf course up near Blair Estate. They often visited the public park and the route they took was past the 'seik hoose' [fever hospital].

The 'Seik Hoose' or Cottage Hospital. Photo courtesy of Robert Barr.

THE DALRY RAWS

Horses passing through Dalry, pulling goods from Glasgow would be taken to the ford in the Rye for a drink of water. The place can be seen in the photo, 'Ford in the Rye water'.

People from Carsehead walked up past the creamery if they were going somewhere on the train.

She remembers swimming in the 'burn' [River Garnock] at 'the tail of the rat'. [Replies to local enquiries and discussion on the local Facebook page produced a majority view that the place was actually the 'tail of the Rye' where the Rye Water joins the river Garnock. Local fishermen especially are familiar with names for stretches of river and provided the location indicated on the map, 'Tail of

Ford on the Rye Water in 2022, photo by the author.

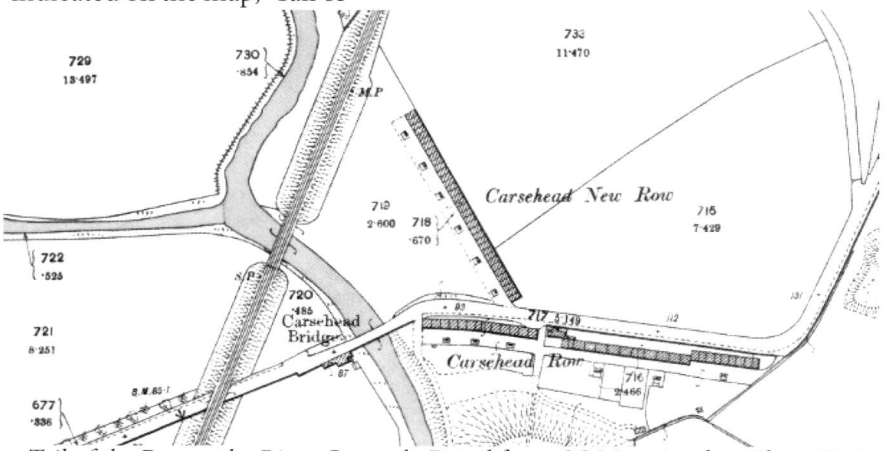

Tail of the Rye on the River Garnock. Detail from OS Map, Ayrshire Sheet XI.4 Revised 1909, Published 1910, Scale 25 inches: 1 mile, reproduced with the permission of the National Library of Scotland,

- Present day photograph of the Tail of the Rye on the River Garnock (phot by the author).

the Rye on the Garnock River'. The map illustrates its proximity to Carsehead.]

The boys swam further up and threw in pennies and halfpennies and dived in to retrieve them. She was allowed to go swimming when she was about 10 years old. She remembers Sunday School trips on buses to Saltcoats or Stevenston. She went to Courthill Church, (now Trinity) and 'The Brethren' [a Protestant Evangelical religious movement]. She also remembers the Sunday School trip to the Blair Estate. On a Sunday night she would often walk round the Loans. One of the neighbours, Alec Houston, used to take a crowd of weans to walk over the Fairlie Moor to Fairlie. Sometimes they walked back and sometimes they got the train. Alec worked for the electricity board, but electricity had not been installed in his own house.

Ella said there was a great community spirit in Carsehead Raw. There was a neighbour who had had a leg amputated and all the other mothers helped her with washing. (In fact, they helped everyone with washing, offering their neighbours left over hot water and so on.) This lady was a beautiful knitter and knitted shawls for babies when she heard a baby was on the way. Doors were never locked and adults would chap [knock], open neighbours' doors and enter their houses. Raws folk were all kind and if you ran out of anything you just had to say and someone would lend you what you needed. If neighbours noticed that your door was not open by a certain time in the morning they'd check everything was okay. Before the National Health Service, someone came round all the houses on a Saturday morning and collected 2s 6d [12½p] from every family. This entitled them to call the doctor if anyone in the family was ill and to free prescriptions if required. If neighbours saw the doctor calling at a house, a neighbour would call in when he had left to find out who was ill and offer to do anything to help, such as taking a prescription to the chemist. At that

THE DALRY RAWS

Drakemyre with Lodging House first building on the right. Photo courtesy of Pollacchi family.

time, the chemists in Dalry were Loudon and Knowles.

Whoever was up first got everybody's newspaper, and often men coming home from night shift would bring neighbours' newspapers too.

Ella's Mother was always busy. She made sure they did their homework, washed their hair on Sunday and if you so much as scratched your head the bone comb came out [to search for head lice.] If her mother had visitors the weans had to be seen and not heard. Her mother hand sewed quilts from old dresses and used a hand sewing machine to make school skirts and kimonos. Ella remembers the smell of scones baking at her granny's on a Sunday morning. Food was plain but they were always well fed. There was always soup and if there were enough coupons for butcher meat they got mince with potatoes and veg and sometimes a sweet. The raws people were kind to outsiders too. The people from the lodging house at Drakemyre came round with their 'tinnies' and were given a cup of tea and something to eat. [A lodging house was a kind of hostel with very basic facilities for itinerant workers, vagrants and the less fortunate members of society.] It can be seen in the photo of the 'Lodging House'.

Round about the raws there were several places of work. Nearby was the 'killing hoose' or slaughterhouse, where the Co-op, McClymonts and Marshalls all butchered their animals two or three times a week. Fleming and Reid's Mill was nearby and Ella put her name down there when they visited the school to recruit school leavers. The photo, 'Earlier photo of

THE DALRY RAWS

Earlier photo of New Street with Fleming and Reid mill in the distance. Photo courtesy of Armour Hamilton.

New Street with Fleming and Reid's Mill in the distance' shows the mill from near the junction of New Street and Garnock Street.

Her friend, Myra Cairns, had left school the previous February and started in Fleming and Reid's but one Sunday night her brother asked her to go for chips. She went on her bike and coming back, someone spoke to her, she turned round and crashed with a bus. She was killed in the collision. Ella had been meant to start work with her at the mill and this made her wonder whether she should still take up the offer of a job since Myra would not be there, but in the end, she did start work there and she got on well. She left school on the Friday and started work there on the Monday at the age of 14. Her job was locking, involved in making socks, also operating the linking machine across the toes and a machine to put tartan across the top.

She worked from 7am – 5pm with one hour for lunch and often Tom Reid, the milkman, gave 6 -10 young women a lift home at lunch time piled into the back of his horse drawn milk cart. The manager of the mill was Jimmy McCrae and he lived in Tofts Cottage. There was an Italian prisoner of war camp nearby during the Second World War and the prisoners teased them and threw snowballs in winter. Ella continued to work at the mill until she left to have her first baby. Her husband was Wullie Cairns and he was a miner, like his father before him. There were no pit-head showers and Wullie had to wash in the house at the end of every shift. Ella washed his pit clothes. They lived in Vennel Street then got a brand-new council house in Baidland Avenue in 1954. This made it easier for Wullie to clean up after a shift and for Ella to wash his working clothes. Wullie worked at

THE DALRY RAWS

Carsehead Raw deserted and awaiting demolition, photo courtesy of Robert Barr.

Douglas mine, Blair and Lockwood. One advantage of being a miner was that they got free coal. He tried to sign up for the army during the war, but mining was a reserved occupation, so he was not accepted. He tried to get different jobs when he was 35 but he was told that he was too old. Ella thinks that the employers didn't want to take on an ex-miner. Eventually when the mines closed he got a job in Broadlie brickworks.

When her mother moved out of Carsehead Raw someone else moved in until they in turn were allocated a council house. The Carsehead Raws were last to be emptied and demolished because they were of a better standard than many others. A lot of people who lived there moved abroad. Ella missed the raw because you knew everybody and everybody knew you. It was not the same moving into a scheme.

Ella could remember the names of most of the neighbours:

Miller, Stirling, Chapman, Davidson, Hill, Borland, Houston, Cairns, Jackie Lyndsay, Anderson, Houston, McInnes, McMillan, Cox, McInnes, Harry Miller, Crewlands who kept hens, 'the corner', Caigs, Paterson, Houston, Marley, Andrews, Roddie, Miller, Andrews, Morgan, Burns [her family], Harvey, Rae, McClure. This is 30 out of 33 families. [I have compared Ella's list with the names on the 1935 and 1940 valuation rolls and all of the names she mentions appear on at least one of the rolls, often with runs of six or more families in the same order as in the rolls.]

THE DALRY RAWS

Jana Drummond Dippie

Jana was born in 23 Carsehead Row in 1945. Her great grandparents had originally lived across the road in the 'Torry Raw' where the floors were beaten earth and the roof was covered with tarred felt. Her maternal grandfather had been born at Torry Raw but later he lived at 23 Carsehead Row with Jana's grandmother and when her parents were first married they lived with them. Jana believes that at one time an aunt and a couple of uncles also stayed there at the same time. Her mother's maiden name was Houston. Jana was able to provide several photographs taken outside Carsehead Raws.

Jana Drummond Dippie

Later her grandparents were rehoused to a council house in Craig Avenue and later still Mair Avenue and it was just Jana, her sister and parents who lived at Carsehead. They had no electricity or running water in the house. There were stone floors with rag rugs everywhere which

Jana Drummond Dippie's great grandfather at the door of Carsehead Row, all photos courtesy of Jana Drummond Dippie.

had been made by her granny and mother. There was an entry hall and the kitchen had two sinks, one for drainage and one for storing water. This was carried into the house several times a day in a blue bucket from the pump outside. This pump was decorated with a big lion's head. Jana remembers that her grandparents had cooked on a range in the main room, but her mother had a gas cooker in the kitchen. The gas pressure was low, and it took a long time to cook anything. It was really too low to cook chips, which require a high heat. Jana remembers being reluctant to eat chips cooked on the gas cooker because she said that they had come out like white slugs. They were however made to eat everything because money was short.

Jana Drummond Dippie's grandfather with his first motor bike and the rows in the background.

The Drummonds can be traced back to Aberdeenshire originally. Jana's paternal grandfather had worked as a railway engineer and moved around a lot. He had nine children, and they were each born in a different town. Her father was born in Airdrie but the family later moved to Lochwinnoch. Jana's father was orphaned at two years old and was brought up by his older brothers and sisters. When he left school he started an apprenticeship as a metal polisher and at the same time her mother was working in the office of Fleming and Reid's mill but they both received Essential Work Orders during the war requiring them to work at the 'Dynamite', later called Ardeer or ICI, in Stevenston. This was part of the war effort and they met when they were both working at ICI. Her father was later called up to the Royal Navy. Her parents married in 1944 and after the war he couldn't return to his apprenticeship so he started working in the Barytes mine outside Lochwinnoch. He had only been there for two weeks when there was an accident resulting in one man dying and Jana's father's leg being crushed. He couldn't work for four years and was unemployed so that is why money was tight. Her mother worked night shifts in the office of the brickworks to earn some money. Eventually her father had his leg amputated.

Jana described the bottom row and the middle row with a gap

between, which was called 'the corner'. Middle row and top row were joined but one was set back so that they were not absolutely aligned. The living room had a set-in bed backing onto the kitchen, but when Jana stayed there the set-in bed was not used. Later the range was removed and her parents had a modern fireplace installed which had two seats built into the surround. There was a big bedroom which had a fireplace. Jana was born in that room, as was her mother. Previously, because her grandfather had been a coal miner, they had access to cheap coal so the fire was lit in winter but her parents could not afford so much coal so it was only lit if someone was ill in bed.

Jana Drummond Dippie (standing) and her sister in the arms of an unknown relative outside Carsehead Raws.

There was a small bedroom looking onto Beith Road which had a double bed and a chest of drawers. There was not enough room for more furniture. Jana and her sister used to lie in bed looking at the shapes and patterns on the ceiling, believing them to be like maps of foreign countries but she realises now that they were likely to be damp patches.

Jana remembers that one of their neighbours was Bulger Marley, there were Houstons, Caigs, and her violin teacher, Mr Miller.

Outside, there was a communal wash house shared by 12 families. Each family was allocated half a day each week. There was a boiler which had a fire lit underneath to heat the water. When the water was hot enough, the wooden lid was removed and the clothes put into the boiler to wash with soap powder. There were two huge deep sinks, with washing boards where some clothes were washed with Sunlight Soap. The floor became soaking wet and Jana remembers splashing about in it wearing wellies and can still smell the suds. The clothes were wrung out by passing through a giant wringer or mangle.

There were sixteen flush toilets attached to the wash houses with two families sharing each toilet. They used squares of newspaper hung

THE DALRY RAWS

up with string as toilet paper. Some families stored various things in the toilets. One family kept a cage of ferrets in their shared toilet. If you needed the toilet during the night you used a potty which would be emptied in the morning. Jana's mother worked hard keeping the toilet clean.

For personal washing, people had a stand-up wash at the sink and once a week had a bath in the house. Water for this was heated on the gas cooker. It took a very long time and children were washed in a small quantity of water shared by any brothers and sisters!

Jana's grandfather was a miner in Lochwood Mine and he came home black from coal dust but he seemed to wash to the waist only each day and to have a bath once a week.

Jana Drummond Dippie playing outside Carsehead Rows with the wash houses in the background.

Jana Drummond Dippie's maternal grandfather, James Houston in the back garden of 80 Mair Avenue after a shift at Lochwood Mine, his face covered in coal dust.

Outside the Row was a blaes road with the pump and wash house. The blaes was waste from mining. Beyond that were long gardens which some people tended and others didn't bother with. Jana remembers a corrugated iron fence which had been painted with tar. In the summer this melted and the children picked bits off and chewed it then spat it out like chewing gum.

Jana has happy memories of being outside playing in the 'holla' [hollow], at kick the can, and sliding down the bing which was blaes and made them filthy. She remembers playing houses and laying out lines of small stones to demarcate her 'house'. She also picked wildflowers and pretended to sell them in her 'shop'. They went swimming in the ha'penny hole. This was a natural swimming place in the River Garnock which had shallow places to paddle and a deeper bit where children learned to swim. Men had put a diving board over the deep bit. [Local people have described this to me as being a little further upstream from the tail of the rat/Rye' mentioned by Ella Burns and may have been the place she described as being where older boys swam.]

Her grandfather made bicycles from scrap metal and the whole family would cycle to the coast.

Although she has happy memories of her time in the raws, there are also unhappy memories of domestic abuse going on in other families. Jana left when she was eight and moved to Stoopshill Crescent. She attended Dalry Primary School and Dalry High then trained as a teacher and returned to teach at Dalry Primary School. She is married, lives in Dalry and has one daughter.

Sadie McGinnes Hamilton

I did not interview Sadie directly because her family felt it would be too tiring for her, so I gave them a list of questions and they asked her these over several days. This is a summary of her replies.

Sadie was born in 1925 at number 18 Carsehead Row also known as 'Sticket Row'. Her father was the supervisor in the slaughterhouse.

Sadie said that inside the raw there was a living room and a bedroom. The top raw houses had one bedroom and the bottom raw had two. They were in the second top house. There were carpets and linoleum on the floor and wallpaper on the walls. They had easy chairs, a kitchen table and a range-type fire. There were gas lights. They had one gas ring and they also put pots on the fire to cook. There was no oven, but they could make scones on a griddle on the gas ring. They were the only house with running water.

Outside, the raws were painted white. There was a wash house shared by six houses and there were gardens at the back. Some people kept hens. Their neighbours were the Millers and Coxs. The fathers in these families worked in the steelworks and mines. She also remembers Mrs Morgan who was a great knitter and walked with crutches. There was also W. Marley who was a chimney sweep.

Sadie liked the friendship among the people who lived in the raws but the thing she liked least were the outside toilets.

She remembers having her teeth pulled by Dr Watt and the district nurse on the kitchen table in the living room. She also had to go to Ayr to have her tonsils out when she was about 11. A funny memory is when sheep escaped from the 'killing hoose' and the men had to help catch them. She also remembers Maud McMillan going to the wash house with her toothbrush and toothpaste to brush her teeth. A sad memory is Myra Cairns being killed in an accident when she was riding her bike.

Sadie went to Dalry Primary School and High School and when she left school she worked in a sweetie shop for six months then became a nursery nurse at Dalry Nursery. Later she went to the 'Dough School' and became the cook for the nursery along with Mrs Close. [The Dough School was the affectionate nickname for the then Domestic Science College in Glasgow.]

Sadie left Carsehead when she was 25, moving to Vennel Street. When the rest of the family moved out to a new house in the Blair Scheme they were quite happy to leave Carsehead.

Sadie can remember all the families who lived in the raws at that time. In the first row were: J. Miller, Clelland, H. Miller, D. McGinnes [her father], J. Cox, McMillans, Lindsays, J. Beaton, D. McInnes, A. Houston, W. Dunn, Houston, Cairns (Myra's family), Houston, Borland, Hill, Stirling, Davidson, Jean Chapman and W. Miller.

In the second row were: Caig, Drummonds [including Jana later on], Houston, Andrews, Palmer, Andrews, Morgan, Rae and McClure. [As with Ella Burns, Sadie's memory of the families in Carsehead can be confirmed by the valuation rolls of the time.]

Alex Harkins

Alex was born in 1943 in Single Raw and the family later moved to Furnace Raw. He lived in the Peesweep until he was 12 years old when they moved to Cleeves Avenue as the first tenants in a brand-new council house. There were four children in the family, all boys. Alex's three brothers were Jim, Archie and John.

There are a lot of people called Harkins in Dalry, partly because Alex's father's youngest brother had eight sons. At one time his uncle, aunt and their eight sons all lived in a two-bedroom house in Burnhouse Avenue.

Alex described the inside of Furnace Raw. There was one room with two recessed beds, end to end along one wall. The front door opened straight into the room and there was a window at the front. At the back there was a small area curtained off as a scullery. It had a window in it but was not really used much as it was very damp.

The boys used to play by jumping onto the sprung recessed beds and one day his youngest brother, Jim, injured his hip bone by doing this. The bone became diseased and caused Jim to limp as time passed. It was realised that the hip bone had stopped growing and the treatment was for Jim to remain in a special frame in Killearn Hospital near Stirling for one year and seven months. Alex's father took him to visit his brother about once a month.

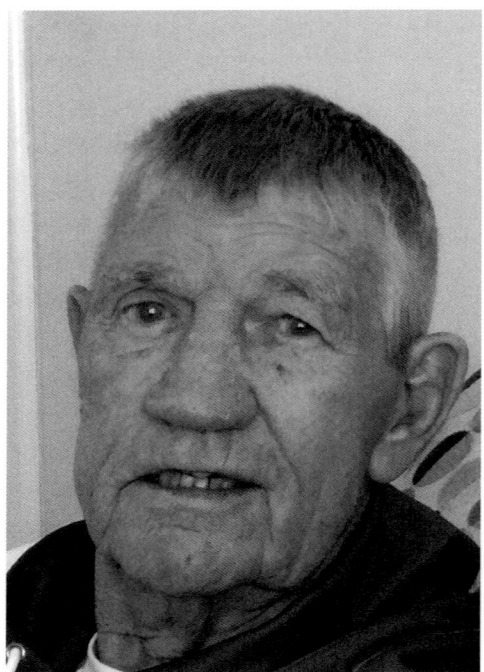

Alex Harkins

Furnace Raw was the biggest raw. Alex also remembered Front Raw which was also called Turned Raw because it faced away from Blair Road. This was said to be because Lady Blair did not want to see the poverty of the people who lived in the raws as she frequently passed by on her way from the Blair Estate to the town and back. Alex wondered why Single Raw was so named because the houses were built back-to-back. He did not remember Double Raw when I asked.

Alex could remember who lived in most of the houses in Furnace Raw as follows:

Number 1 - Eilan Skeogh who fenced off her garden and kept a couple of geese which were very aggressive; No 2 - a man who had lost his legs in the war and drove a specially adapted Mini Minor car; No 3 - Lizzie Clark who had a lot of lasses; No 4 - Harkins; No 5 - Jeanie Simpson McGoogan; No 6 - Jeanie's sister Maran Simpson; No 7 - Mary Fleck Higgins; No 8 - Granny Harkins; No 9 - Dunlop; No 10 - Beattie; No 11 - ?, No 12 - ?, No 13 - Uncle Archie and Auntie Betty Harkins who later had eight boys. (She did French polishing in her living room, having served her time to learn it.); No 14 - ?, No 15 - Rita Ross who ran a shop from her house, No 16 - Morrison [the family of James who has also contributed to this oral history.]

THE DALRY RAWS

Alex and I compared his list to the valuation roll for 1940/1941 and many people on the roll were in the same houses several years later when Alex remembered his neighbours. It is also interesting to note that he had several relatives living in the same raw – a common occurrence which was likely to contribute to the close community ties for which the raws were famous.

He described the position of wash houses with flush toilets attached. Each toilet was shared by four or five families, and he remembered toilet paper consisted of scraps of newspaper on a six-inch nail. Water for the weekly bath came from the wash house and was heated in a pot over the fire in the house then poured into the zinc bath. Alex went first because he was the oldest and his younger brothers went in after him.

Alex remembered a park where they played football.

He mentioned the special closeness between the people in Peesweep. They helped each other and you could always ask a neighbour to borrow some sugar or a few slices of bread. They were poor – Alex said, 'they had nothing'. For this reason, he remembered that people stole potatoes, carrots and turnips from farmers' fields and caught rabbits and pheasants in snares. Food acquired in this way would be shared among the neighbours. He remembered one man stole 48 chickens from a farm and carried them home in a pram, intending to distribute them among neighbours. He put them in the wash house but he was caught and sentenced to six months in Barlinnie Prison. While he was in prison he learned cobblery and was later able to repair shoes for all his family and many neighbours.

Another time, a man had stolen a bag of coal from the Brickworks and was manoeuvring it into his house through the back window in Furnace Raw. This raw backed onto a very steep slope down towards the foundry and he lost his balance and fell a long distance down the slope. There were children round about who thought it very funny but the man had got a terrible fright and did not think it funny so the children knew better than to laugh.

One day when Alex was ten, he was walking on the Stoopshill bing across from Blairlands farm with his brothers and his mother. They heard the horns of the Blair hunt. A fox ran past Alex and he was terrified that the hounds would follow, so afraid that he had the strength to jump a four-foot fence, shouting, 'Mammy! Mammy!'

Alex's father had two jobs: he worked in the brickworks and as a barman in the Royal Hotel two nights a week. Alex started doing part-time jobs himself as soon as he was able. When he was at primary school, during the school summer holidays he pedalled an ice cream tricycle from the Italian café to the Peesweep. He wasn't strong enough to pedal up the hill and had to get off and push. He pedalled round the raws and sold ice cream cones. At the weekends, he looked after the snooker room behind the same café, later called the Station Café. He wrote down start and finish times on a board and took in the money. [I asked him how he could handle money when he was so young, but he said with a laugh that he has always understood money.]

When he was a little older he had a paper run delivering the *Evening Citizen* to the Lynn scheme and the pubs and also did a milk run with Jimmy Hair on his horse and cart. He helped Ramages the fruit merchant on a Friday night when his lorry came to the Peesweep, selling apples, oranges, bananas, peaches and grapes. Alex's main duty was to ensure no-one stole the goods while the driver served other customers. For that he got a few pennies or a bunch of free fruit. When he was in his final year of primary school he did a milk run on the Co-operative milk lorry driven by Jock Gordon in the morning before school, delivering milk and rolls round Garnock Street and the Lynn Scheme. He started at 6am, helping to load up the van outside the bakery in Smith Street and he finished at 8.50, just in time to get to school for 9am. He continued with this job when he went to the higher-grade school. He gave all the money he earned from these various jobs to his mother. There were times when Alex was earning more than his father who earned about £3 10s while Alex could earn £1 10s from 2 days at the snooker alone.

When Alex was ten his father went to Canada to find a job and accommodation, then eighteen months later the rest of the family joined him, but Alex did not like Canada at first, so he came back to Scotland and stayed with his granny in Garnock Street. In fact, the whole family moved back and forth between Scotland and Canada at various times. At one time his mother worked as a conductress on the SMT buses then on Paterson buses when they started a local run. She also used to charter a bus from Paterson's for day trips to the beach, usually Seamill. She took bookings in advance and a whole coach-load of families from Peesweep would travel together to the shore for the day. They had sing-songs on the bus and races on the shore. Alex remembered the three-legged race in particular and said that they were great times.

Around this time the raws were being demolished and Alex remembers groups of men stripping the lead from gas pipes to the empty houses as well as from the roofs. This was transported to a scrap dealer in Kilmarnock and the money divided between the men.

When Alex was thirteen and his mother was in Scotland and his father in Canada he started going to a 'Tossing School' at the Lovers' Walk next to the River Garnock in Dalry. This was an illegal gambling meeting where men bet on the fall of two pennies, two heads or two tails winning. Look-outs were posted to warn if the police approached. Around 30 or 40 men, maybe more, from all around the towns of Dalry, Kilbirnie, Beith, Kilwinning and Dunlop congregated every Sunday afternoon. To everyone's amazement Alex won £360. His uncle Jim was there and helped himself to £30 of Alex's winnings. He walked Alex home to make sure no-one tried to steal his winnings. Alex hid most of the money in the house then took about £30 to the Station Café where Alex had previously had part time jobs. A group of young people gathered and Alex was dancing to the juke box with the lassies from the mill and buying everyone fish suppers. Someone went and told Alex's mother who hotfooted it to the café, took Alex home and took the remaining money from Alex – about £300. He told her that his uncle had taken £30 from him so she went to her brother-in-law's house and demanded that money back.

He said that there was not much socialising between the people from Peesweep and Carsehead although he was friendly with Tam Caig who lived there. He also remembered the slaughterhouse at Carsehead.

When he was fifteen years old he left school and started working in Finlay's Brickwork. [This is named Carsehead Brickwork on various industrial history websites, but Alex had never heard it called Carsehead. It was always known as Finlay's to his knowledge.]   His father was back in Scotland at that time and also worked there along with Alex's uncle Patsy. His uncle died in an industrial accident in the brickworks on a day when Alex was working although he did not see the incident. Alex worked in the most unpleasant part of the brickworks called the 'stoorie laft' [dusty loft] where material from the bing which had been crushed was riddled to remove over-large pieces.

Before he was seventeen years old Alex returned to Canada and joined the Canadian Black Watch regiment on his seventeenth birthday, hoping to serve in Germany, but his battalion remained in Toronto. In his early teens Alex had liked to attend the boxing gym in James Street, Dalry, and he won the Canadian Black Watch Boxing championship. He left three months before his twentieth birthday. He met his wife, Marilyn, and she joined in the to-ing and fro-ing between Scotland and Canada for the next 50-plus years. When in Canada Alex worked in the Yukon and Alaska laying oil pipes and when in Scotland he ran a taxi business. He has a son and a daughter and four grandchildren in Canada.

Mary Watters McInnes

Mary never lived in the raws but lived nearby. As a child she spent a lot of time playing with friends who lived in the Peesweep Raws. She was born in 1919 in North Street, next door to the church.

The Martin family lived next door and Andrew Martin worked in the Co-op hardware shop. Mary had eight brothers and sisters and she was the second youngest with the youngest being George.   Her father worked in Glengarnock Steelworks but he died young, leaving her mother to bring

THE DALRY RAWS

North Street church and house next door where Mary Watters McInnes was born. Photo courtesy of Pollacchi family.

up the family.

Mary had two older brothers, Robert and Jim, who worked as gardeners under Mr Fairlie who was the head gardener in the Blair Estate. Through Robert and Jim working for Colonel and Mrs Blair, Mary's mother was given the use of the gatehouse, North Lodge. In return for living there, the family had to open and close the gates when the Blairs' horse and carriage passed through. Her mother also cleared up horse droppings and kept the driveway near the gates tidy and raked. Later when they had a motor car, the Blairs would sound the horn and someone from the family would run out and open and close the gates. North Lodge was a very good house and the Colonel, Mrs and Miss Blair were said by Mary to be very good people. The only drawback to the house was, she said that there was no plumbed-in bath and the toilet was a dry closet at the end of the garden. Mary's brother, Robert married Sarah Jamieson and Jim married Violet. Violet's father was the green keeper at the golf course on Blair Road and her family lived in a wee house next to the course.

Jim and Violet moved into a house in the Blair Estate which was always known as 'Geordie Seemon's [Simmons] hoose'. Violet worked in the big house; there were about four servants then.

In the summer Mary and some of her brothers and sisters helped pick berries in the walled garden. Mr Fairlie would say, 'Keep singin then I know you're no eatin the berries'. His son became a doctor. Mary remembers the smithy working at the Kilwinning side of the estate. The McMillan family lived in the South Lodge. The grounds were open to the public.

Mary attended primary school in Townend Street, in a building which later became part of the Post Office. Miss Chalmers was her teacher. She was of farming stock. When Mary left school she started work in the mill and later when she was married she lived in Wingfaulds Avenue.

Walking down Blair Road from Mary's house, the first raw was the Big Raw, 'It was a great raw.' Families who lived there who Mary remembers were: Tom McCrae, Sanders, Dick Caig and Rosemary Haylie. The raw facing on Blair Road was Turned Raw,

'There was always fighting at Turned Raw. The next raw you came to was Front Raw and Furnace Raw was over the back, near the water and the bing'.

Mary forgets the name of the raw facing the Big Raw, but Sammy Robb, lived there. This was the raw facing Stoopshill Raw. Lizzie Wilson lived in Turned Raw, Aggie Crawford was in the Front Raw – she was the midwife.

All the doors were unlocked and neighbours just knocked and walked into each other's houses. Mary's friends all lived in the raws and her mother 'checked' [chastised] her for always being at the Peesweep. She remembers Robert Sanders, Peggy Sanders, also the Haylies who stayed near the middle of the raw. Rosemary Haylie used to go to the water pump wearing her dressing gown. Because there was no running water in the raws, people bathed in a bine full of water which came from the outside pump.

The houses had two rooms and some looked out over the golf course.

To wash clothes you had to set the fire in the wash house on a Friday night. On Saturday morning, it was lit and the washing done in the wash house.

There was a railway ran from Douglas's brickwork, across Blair Road and up to Number 9 pit.

Mary remembers a hall where you could have a wedding reception or a meeting near the Furnace Raw. She can't remember what it was called. There were gas streetlights, switched on by Tom McCrae when it became dark.

Recently as the oldest resident in Dalry she was a guest at the official opening of the A737 Dalry Bypass.

Mary latterly lived in Kilwinning with her daughter.

THE DALRY RAWS

Betty Simpson McManus

Betty was born in 13 New Single Row in 1939. She had two sisters and a brother. Her sisters, Nancy/Agnes and Nellie were older and helped to look after her.

There was no running water in the house and she remembers being bathed in the 'bine' in the wash house. The water was heated up in a boiler then moved into the bine.

There was a day for washing and a day for having a bath too. The family all had a bath on the same night. Water for the house also came from the wash house. There were drying greens and clothes poles at the back.

Betty Simpson McManus

The toilets were outside across the road and there was also a coal house outside. The road between the raws was narrow. The house was a single end with two built-in beds. She slept in a bed chair, her parents slept in one set-in bed, her brother and sister in the other and her older sister slept in their grandparents' house in Furnace Raw.

There was a gas cooker and gas lights and a coal fire. She loved the coal fire and misses it now. The floor was cement with linoleum and rugs on top.

Her father was a railway ganger. Her mother was a scullery maid in Motherwell before she moved to Dalry. She did her best to keep the place clean. Betty described these times as 'hard days'. They had a lot of porridge and soup made with kale which she remarked is coming into fashion again. She remembered her mother was good at baking Eve's pudding. They had saps [bread moistened with warm milk.] Betty pointed out that 'A lot of people now don't know what saps are.'

When she was a wee girl she played outside the raws with other children, making wee houses, playing with dock leaves and there was a big old-fashioned rocking horse which belonged to her cousin who lived in the same raw. One of the neighbours, Harry Welsh, made Betty a doll's house. They would get a jam jar of water and put in rose petals to make 'perfume'. They also played on the Stoopshill bing, really a huge pile of waste from the mines.

THE DALRY RAWS

The 1st tee at Dalry Golf Course, photo courtesy of Robert Barr. Photo enhanced by Hugh Anderson.

She remembers going on the Sunday School trip to the Blair Estate. There would be four or five Clydesdale horses and carts provided by St Margaret's Church and the children tried to pick the best decorated cart. There used to be peacocks in the grounds and there was a market garden in the Blair Estate where you could pick your own strawberries.

Her grandfather looked after the golf course across the road from the Blair Estate gates [North Lodge.]

There was a shop run by Billy Rose in the raws selling things like tins of soup and sweeties. Betty remembers Minnie Gallacher and the Roddie family from the raws.

When she was five years old, they moved to Wingfaulds Avenue. Some neighbours from New Single Row, the Longs and the Crawfords, moved to Wingfaulds Avenue at the same time. When they moved there 'it was like heaven, having three bedrooms and a bathroom.' Her father, her brother Ted, and she went a walk up the Baidland Hill every Sunday. They did all the walks like the Velvet Path.

Her older sister worked in a shoe shop but was called up to the Auxiliary Territorial Service during the war. Her brother, Ted Simpson, worked in the Co-op hardware. When Betty left school she worked in the dyeworks as a wool examiner. After she was married she continued to work for about a year until she got pregnant. She met her husband because he was a friend of her brother's. They used to go on the bus to the dancing in the Walker Hall in Kilbirnie. When they were married at first, they lived in James Street then moved to Parkhill Drive. In fact her husband was a bricklayer employed by Malcolm McManus at the time and helped to build her current house. Later he owned several shops and was a fish monger. Betty described him as 'an entrepreneur'.

AGNES SLAVIN MAXWELL

Agnes was born in 1939 and she remembers the raws because her granny had previously lived in Stoopshill Raw and used to take Agnes to visit her old neighbours. Agnes's mother was brought up there until they were among the first to move out to Merksworth Avenue. Her granny had grown-up sons contributing to the household finances so she could afford the rent, but some people refused a council house because the rents were too high. Later in the 1950s when people moved out of the raws, the houses were not demolished right away and other people moved in for a while, until eventually they had to move out because the houses were being demolished. When older people moved out sometimes younger families moved in, and they did the houses up. Sometimes married sons or daughters with their children moved in to be with elderly relatives and this led to overcrowding.

Agnes's parents were allocated a council house on Blair Road in 1951 when she was twelve years old and the raws were still standing directly across the road.

The Peesweep Raws were on the Beith side of Blair Road. On the right-hand side of Blair Road were farmers' fields until 1951 when council houses on this side started to be built to accommodate people in substandard private lets. She had lived in 10 Garnock Street before moving to Blair Road. The house in Garnock Street had been overcrowded and her mother hung a curtain to separate the sisters and brothers in the bedroom. You had to go downstairs to get water from the outside tap.

When married, Agnes and her husband lived with her parents in Blair Road, then they were allocated a house of their own in Stoopshill Crescent. Later they swapped houses with her parents to

Agnes Slavin Maxwell

get a bigger house since her parents no longer needed a big house and the smaller one suited them. Thus, Agnes has lived in the same house since she was 12 except for a short time in Stoopshill Crescent.

Agnes remembers the Agricultural houses on the opposite side from the raws. She remembers Big Raw which possibly was officially called Blair Row, Turned Raw, Furnace Raw over near the bing, Double Raw where the houses were built back-to-back, and Stoopshill Raw which was sometimes called the Back Raw. She remembers a water pump outside the Big Raw but she is unsure if it was still in use at that time. Some of the houses were empty because the residents had been allocated a council house either in the town or Blair scheme and no-one had moved in in their place. The Big Raw was the first raw to be knocked down while people still lived in the Turned Raw.

Agnes remembers the women sitting on the steps knitting and blethering. The women in the town or in the council houses didn't do this. Town women blethered at the back doors while they were hanging out the washing but didn't sit on the front steps. Despite the different social customs of the women from the raws and from the town, Agnes as a town resident respected the standard of cleanliness of the raws' residents as she commented that people kept the raws up to a good standard. They took a lot of pride in their houses. The women scrubbed the steps with a scrubbing brush and a bucket of water. They whitened the steps. They kept the windows nice with net curtains. The houses were not slums.

On the other side of the road in the council houses there was a mixture of people who had moved in from town houses or from the Peesweep Raws across the road.

When the council houses in Blair Road were allocated, the people in the raws felt that they should be first to be allocated the new council houses across the road, but there were people in the town housed in even worse conditions than in the raws, and sometimes they got a council house before the people from the raws. Some people in the raws resented this but Agnes feels that the new council houses were allocated fairly.

The raw on Blair Road had to be kept perfect because the people from the Blair Estate would pass up and down in their pony and carts and later private motors. Miss Blair liked to see the steps whitened. She also didn't like to see the women sitting out on their steps, so on a Sunday they would keep an eye on the time and when it was nearly time for the horse and cart, or later car, to pass on the way to the kirk they would withdraw.

Just across from where Agnes lives now, she remembers rubble on the ground which was left over from the reading room. This was the community centre of its day and people had meetings and weddings in it. Retired miners also gathered in there to pass the time.

The Turned Raw had gas light inside but Agnes doesn't know if any of the other raws had electricity. There were still outside water pumps in 1951 but most houses had running water by then. Outside toilets were shared: five or six toilets to about fifteen houses. Some had toilets at the back.

There were wash houses, each shared by three or four houses. You were allocated a washing day, the same day each week. The man of the house often lit the fire under the boiler first thing in the morning. When the water was boiling the whites, sheets, etc. would be washed, then cold water added for the rest of the wash. At the end you would offer a neighbour any hot water that was left and she might go in and do a hand wash in your left-over water.

People were kind to each other. Agnes remembers her granny saying that during the general strike when she stayed in the raws, when there was little money to buy food, men stole turnips from farmers' fields but would share with a neighbour. They were often fined for it. Likewise, if her grandfather caught fish, he would give some away.

The Blair family owned the land, but the houses belonged to the mine owner. The landlords didn't do much to keep the houses up to standard. The houses were owned by Baird, the mine owners and the rent collector answered to the Bairds. The managers collected the rent.

Agnes said that she remembers the inside of the raws as being very dim at night because they were lit by Tilley lamps. [A type of paraffin lamp.] There were two rooms: 'a room and kitchen'. The room was a bedroom, and the kitchen was kitchen/come living room. The kitchen had a set-in bed, although sometimes this was removed and the space used for a cooker and sink if they had one. The mother, father and youngest child would sleep in the kitchen and everyone else in the bedroom. Some families were large. Some raws had a lobby and some had a wee bit curtained off in the main room for a cooker.

Agnes's younger brother played with the weans from the raws but if there was a falling out or they didn't need him to make up the numbers for football they would tell him to, 'Get ower tae yir ain side o' the road. You get oot o' here, ye don't belang here. You come fae the toon'.

As council houses were completed, the council moved people out of the raws into the council houses, then knocked down the raws until they had all been demolished. Agnes thinks they started knocking the raws down in 1952/3. The first one to go was the Main Raw. The Turned Raw lasted quite a while longer.

There was an in-between time when the council houses in Stoopshill Crescent on the same side as the Raws had been built, but some raws were still standing. Eventually all the raws were demolished and replaced by council houses.

Their neighbours in Blair Road were the Roses and they had run a simple shop in the raws. They continued to do so after they moved into their council house. They sold lemonade, cigarettes and sweeties.

Agnes had been told that there were raws on the outskirts of Dalry as well as at the Peesweep. There were raws up the road towards the main Largs Road.

Agnes's paternal granny had stayed in a raw at the top of Hagthorn Brae between Dalry and Kilbirnie when she was a child. These raws were near Borestone in the parish of Dalry. Borestone was quite self-contained with its own shop. Agnes remembers the ruins of the Borestone Raws. The Hagthorn Raws were in the parish of Kilbirnie so Agnes's granny went to school there although she considered herself to be from Dalry.

A lot of Catholics who had originally come from Ireland lived at Borestone, but there were Catholics living in the Peesweep raws too. The town people in Dalry and Kilbirnie didn't want the Irish.

Agnes's mother and Agnes herself did sewing for the Borwicks and Miss Blair on the Blair Estate.

Agnes's granny made herbal remedies and assisted the doctor when he did minor operations on people's kitchen tables, and she kept white linen sheets for the operations. The doctor would tell her when she was needed and she helped at childbirths too. Agnes's granny would help people out including taking in people who were new to the town and had nowhere to stay. The priest would announce from the pulpit at Mass on Sunday if a young woman needed lodgings and Agnes's granny would take her in. Agnes said that there wouldn't have been much room and she perhaps had to sleep on the floor with a blanket over her but at least it was a roof over her head until she found something better.

When Agnes left school she started work in a tailor's premises in Love Lane. She later married and when she had children she no longer worked at the tailor's but continued to sew for the family and for private customers.

JAMES MORRISON

James was born in his grandfather's house at 18 Furnace Row in 1950 in a set-in bed. He was named after his grandfather who was known as Jimmock. He had fought in the Boer War and the First World War and died in 1968, aged 93. Living in the single end were his grandfather, parents and sister Jean, seven years older than James. His grandmother, Martha McCully had been a midwife. James was Dr Wilson's first delivery. James remembers gas mantles and that there was no electricity or running water in the raws. Their neighbour was Vera Campbell.

His grandfather worked in Finlay Brickworks, but he had previously been a miner. Lots of men in Dalry had originally been miners, but when the pits closed they either moved away or started work in the brickworks. James remembers that lots of women worked in the big mill, Fleming and Reid's. 'It was huge'.

The family moved to a brand-new council house at 13 Cleeves Avenue in 1955. Bobby Hately was the county councillor and could help you get a council house. James shared a room with his grandfather, his sister had a room and his parents had a room. Nearby neighbours in Cleeves Avenue were the Friels, Higgenses and Townsleys.

James Morrison

James's family's house backed onto the Maxwells' back garden.

James remembers the raws being demolished and when he lived in Cleeves Avenue they were still building Baidland Avenue. There was a big lime pit across from where Paterson's garage was. The lime was used in the building of the houses. One day when he was seven or eight, while playing, James fell in and boys had to get an adult to pull him out by the neck, then he had to go home and get all the lime washed off.

On Mother's Day he would go up to the Blair Estate and pick a big armful of daffodils for his mother. She would be horrified and tell him off. He went up to Kilpatrick farm to buy milk, cream, eggs and buttermilk.

James remembers police houses on the left-hand side at the top of Stoopshill Crescent. These were a few council houses set aside exclusively for tenants who were police officers. Jack Warden was a policeman who lived in there when James was young and his daughter Moira went to school with James's sister, Jean.

James's first job on leaving school was building chicken houses out of asbestos, then he worked in Glengarnock steelworks doing a dangerous job in the melting shop, working with molten steel with only an overall and steel toe-capped boots as safety equipment. He was made redundant and started working in ICI when he was married, but twice someone on the opposite shift as James was killed and he decided to leave because it was such dangerous work. He retrained as a chef through a TOPS course [Training

Opportunities course provided by the Department of Employment to improve the employability of unemployed people.] He then worked as a chef in the Laurieston, Ingledene, Kilmeny and Croft hotels, as well as the Garden Grill in Saltcoats. He had five children.

JEAN WATT NIBLOCK

Jean was born Jean Watt in 1940 in 16 Furnace Row and later moved to 9 New Double Row.

Jean was brought up by her mother and grandfather, Rabbie Kirk. Her grandmother had died before she was born. Also in the household were her uncle Bill, (her mother's brother) and her auntie May. However, her auntie May was not a blood relative. She was unofficially adopted into the family in the following way: she was actually the youngest daughter of a neighbouring family called the Thompsons. During the Diphtheria epidemic in 1936, the most seriously ill children were treated in Davidshill hospital, [an infectious diseases hospital situated off the Auchengree Road between Highfield and Longbar.] Davidshill was over-crowded and May's three older brothers all contracted the disease but had to stay at home because the hospital was full. The doctor advised that May should be moved out of the house to prevent her catching Diphtheria. In fact, May's three brothers all died of the disease, as well as a younger brother of Jean's mother. Once the outbreak was over and the house

Jean Watt Niblock

Bill Kirk, all photos courtesy of Jean Watt Niblock.

had been fumigated, May returned to her parents but she never settled. The Kirks missed her, so it was decided that she would return to the Kirk house and Jean's granny looked after her until she died, then Grandpa Kirk took over. Jean was able to supply photographs of her Uncle Bill, his walking stick and her Grandpa Kirk.

Jean's uncle Bill was the only person at Stoopshill Raw to make a garden and before Jean was born, her granny used to make soup from the vegetables he grew and hand a pot of soup into any family where she thought they could use it to feed the weans. Her uncle Bill worked in Ardeer and in his spare time he liked to go walking up into the country at the Fisherman's Brig with a group of friends. They all made walking sticks and Jean still has her uncle Bill's.

Jean Watt Niblock's Uncle Bill's hand-made walking stick, the only object I have seen originating from The Raws.

Jean's mother worked at Fleming and Reid's mill until she had Jean. Her grandpa was a miner at Pit number 7 then later a street sweeper for Ayr County Council. He was well known about the town and she was extremely fond of her grandpa. She used to leave school and run to Smith Street where he was based, to meet him and walk home with him after he finished his work.

Jean has fond memories of growing up in the raws. A lot of folk who didn't experience it have said they 'wouldnae like it', especially having no indoor, plumbed toilet, but she was happy and said she didn't know anything different. There were outside toilets but no running water in the raws and you had to go outside and pump water at the middle of the row. However, Mr McPherson at number 1 Stoopshill Raw was a plumber and installed running water in his house.

Jean mentioned having read information about the raws which stated that there were no wash houses but she specifically remembers her mother going out to the wash house. Also, there is a family story which recounts how one day, when her mother had finished washing the clothes, she thought she would put Jean in for a bath because the left-over water was clean enough. She forgot that there was bleach in the water which made some of Jean's hair fall out, and when it grew back in it was never the same again. She said that you either dried your washing outside or in the living room in front of the range.

When Jean was young she became curious about an object which hung on a nail in the house and asked what it was. She was told it was the key to the door. It was never used and had become rusty with lack of use. This was because people never locked their doors. Jean said, 'and yet there was no burglary'.

There was gas lighting inside the houses and street lighting was by gas too. The 'leerie' (lamp lighter) came round and lit the gas street lighting at night. Jean's auntie May used to climb up the lamp post. Jean said, 'She was a tomboy'.

Jean Watt Niblock's Grandfather, Rabbie Kirk at the door of Stoopshill Raw.

When Jean looks back on the house at New Double Row she thinks people who didn't live there might be surprised to know that they had three bedrooms, although they were all small and all opened off the living room. She described the front door opening into the living room with the kitchen on the right. Beyond the kitchen were two small bedrooms, each with room for a bed and a chest of drawers. The bedrooms had gaps near the ceiling to allow air to circulate. There was an area of the living room partitioned off for a third bedroom. Jean slept in the bedroom with her auntie May, her mother slept in the front bedroom and her grandpa and uncle Bill slept in the back bedroom. Neither her auntie May nor her uncle Bill ever married.

The golf course was at the back of Stoopshill Raw.

Jean remembers Charlotte McIntyre who was a neighbour.

When she was wee Jean played outside a lot, especially with Kathleen Haylie when she was visiting her grandparents who lived nearby. She also played with Gordon Caig. They would all visit her uncle Bill if he was in the garden or generally run about. The girls would play Beds, [a kind of Scottish Hopscotch, also called Peever] but chalk could not be used to mark the unpaved ground and instead, lines and numbers were scraped into the soil. They played with dolls too.

Gordon was her 'knight in shining armour.' At school she was waiting to go into the red building on an icy day and was knocked over by a boy sliding down a slide, sending her flying. She broke her wrist and Gordon hit the boy and said, 'Whit did ye dae that fur?'

Years later she was walking up Blair Road with her future husband and they met Gordon. He said, 'Is this the boyfriend?' Jean said, 'Aye' and Gordon said to him, 'Ye'd better be guid tae her or you'll hae me tae answer tae'. Then Jean's future husband asked if Gordon was an 'ex', but Jean said that he was only a friend. She hadn't had any boyfriends apart from her husband.

Her mother married Jean's step-father, Jian Borzyszkowski, when Jean was six. He was a chef in the Polish army and they moved around a lot to places like Thurso, London and other places in England. Jean often went with them but sometimes she didn't go, and continued to stay behind with her grandpa, aunt May and uncle Bill. Even when she did move, she returned to the raws in between tours of duty. Jean's stepfather left the army when Jean was twelve. He couldn't get a permanent job as a chef, so he worked in the Moorings in Largs in the summer and in Finlay's brickworks in the winter. Eventually he got a permanent job in the Central Hotel in Glasgow and her mother got a job there too. By then they were living in the tenement building at the Highfield.

When her grandpa, aunt May and uncle Bill were allocated a council house in Douglas Avenue, her grandpa was very reluctant to move. Trying to convince and reassure him, the family said, 'You'll have an inside toilet.' He replied, 'There's a toilet oot there.' 'You'll have a bath', 'I'm no boathered aboot a bath.' Eventually, when he realised that he had to move because the raw was being demolished he said, 'Well ah'm takin ma bowl fur ma tea' because he drank tea from a bowl instead of a cup. He smoked a clay pipe. They moved to Douglas Avenue around 1953 and he died around 1955.

Later Jean, her mother and step-father moved to Wingate Avenue and one of their neighbours was the Harkins family who ran the lodging house at Drakemyre.

Jean remembers a song people used to sing:

There is a lodgin hoose, doon Drakemyre Brae
Where they get ham an eggs three times a day,
When they hear the dinner bell, Doon the stairs they run like hell,
Three times a day.

The lodging house was where the Factory Shop is now and where Dalry Motor Company was previously.

When Jean left school she worked in Hannah's shoe shop in Main

Street, then Archie Cochrane's paper shop on The Cross.

After a while, she moved to Robertson's Mill behind where the Factory Shop is now. Her job was mule spinning, tending a huge machine which transferred wool from bobbins to spindles. She had to watch for any breaks and join the wool strands together. Later again she moved to Ardeer, which trebled her wages. However, she had to leave eight weeks after marriage.

One night she went to the Greenbank pub with her husband. She felt self-conscious because women didn't really go to pubs in those days, but her mother said it would do no harm and her husband said it would be nice to go out together as they rarely did. She had a soda and lime then went home. She was 'spotted' by a neighbour and by the time she saw her uncle Bill the next day, he had heard and asked disapprovingly if this was going to be a regular occurrence now. Jean had four children and lives in Kilbirnie now, but she loved living in Dalry, especially at the raws.

[When Kenneth Phillips read a draft of this document it sparked many interesting memories of past Dalry residents. For example, thinking of the lodging house mentioned by Jean and Ella, he remembered that one of the residents at the lodging house was a shell-shocked captain who had been at Dunkirk, and when he had a drink on a Saturday he used to march up and down the bus queues at the Cross shouting out his commands.

He also remembered Jean's auntie May, known as May Keerie who worked at Stoopshill farm doing 'a man's job'. Kenneth also remembers Jean's uncle Bill who worked in Ardeer alongside a relative of Kenneth's called Bladdy Phillips. When Bladdy took a stroke, Bill visited him every Sunday after church, carrying his Bible to spend an hour with Bladdy.]

Elizabeth Davidson Orr

Elizabeth remembers the raws because she was born in 4 Carsehead Row in 1929 and lived there until 1952. Elizabeth understands that the owner, Baird, had promised when these houses were being built that they would be of a high standard with rooms in the attic. In the event, they were only single storeyed and the town folk called them the Sticket Row because he had decided to 'stick at' one storey. The raws folk never called them that. Across the road there had been New Carsehead Row, nicknamed the Tarry Raw because it had tar roofs. Although they were good houses at first, the tar roof deteriorated over the years and so the whole building went downhill.

All the houses were room and kitchens, with two set-in beds in each room, with curtains across although they rarely used them. At first the houses had ranges for heating and cooking, but later fireplaces were installed.

Elizabeth's mother had trivets added so that she could continue to at least boil a kettle on the fire. By this time people also had a gas ring for cooking but the supply was uneven. Later gas cookers were installed and they used the area that had been a set-in bed as a scullery.

The floor was tiled but these were uneven. There were no tiles under the set-in beds and shoes left under there for a few weeks would get damp.

On a fine day, the women took the bed boards outside and washed them. 'You had to watch out for woodworm.' The method was to take four chairs outside and place the bed boards on them to dry. The blankets would be washed the same day.

Elizabeth Orr

There was no running water in the house and it had to be carried in from the wash house. The wash house would be shared by four families. Most preferred a Monday as their wash day but one neighbour preferred a Wednesday, because her daughter worked in a shop and had Wednesday afternoons off so could help her. The wash house had big windows at the back so it was well lit. If the women worked quickly, four families could do the family's weekly wash one after another on the same day. Some women preferred to have the first slot, but others preferred later. The families would joke that these later women were trying to save soap by washing in water used previously with some suds left in it.

In the wash house there was a boiler, a wooden tub for washing, and mangles. The girls went in and had a bath in the same wooden tub the clothes were washed in. The men would also go in at night and have a wash on a different day of the week from the girls and women.

There were big gardens (not always attached to the houses) where tenants grew flowers and vegetables.

Although Carsehead was separate from the Peesweep miners' raws, there was a path connecting them. Elizabeth used to go up there as a child if she had a penny as there was a shop which sold sweeties run by one of the residents in her own home. She also sold other things like kindling. Her mother said people who bought kindling weren't thrifty; her father would go out and collect wood for that purpose. Some of the town people called the people who lived in the Peesweep 'Peesweep Keelies' because a lot of them came originally from Ireland but there were some Irish families in Carsehead Row too.

The people in the raws were very neighbourly and helped each other out. For example, if there was a funeral and a large number of people coming afterwards for tea, the neighbours would lend tablecloths, cups and chairs.

Some people who didn't live in the raws still mention dry closets, as if that is what Elizabeth used, but in her time they always had a flush toilet although it was shared with at least one other family. In Elizabeth's grandfather's time, they did have shared dry closets, but he built a separate one for the family so they didn't have to share in an attempt to avoid TB [tuberculosis] which was rife at the time.

Elizabeth also remembers an outbreak of Diphtheria. One day when she was six years old and at school she took a very sore throat. Coming home from school, her mother wanted to take her to buy new shoes which normally Elizabeth would have been delighted about, but she felt so ill she said she wanted to go straight home so her mother knew she must have been feeling really bad. They met her father coming home from work on his bike and he carried her home on the bike. The next day the doctor came and confirmed what her parents suspected; that she had Diphtheria and she had to go to Davidshill Hospital. The main reason for hospitalization was to contain infection and the only treatment the patients received was breathing moist air from a huge kettle boiling in the ward. They were strapped to their beds to prevent them touching the kettle and accidentally

The Killin' Hoose, or Slaughterhouse, when disused, photo courtesy of Robert Barr.

burning themselves. A teacher gave the children some schoolwork to do. After two weeks, Elizabeth had recovered but many children died, including Myra Ward, [(Robert Ward's sister) and my great uncle, Frank Gallacher.] Houses where someone had the disease had to be 'smeeket' or fumigated and the family had to stay out of the house all day. Elizabeth's family spent the day in the tennis pavilion at the park. This was easy to arrange because her father was the park keeper.

Elizabeth's grandfather was a miner. Her grandmother did not want her sons to be miners, so three of her uncles emigrated to America. By the time Elizabeth was a child, there were not many miners living in Carsehead. At that time there were two tennis courts in Dalry Public Park, one public and one private. When the private one shut down, her father saved the windows from the clubhouse and used them in a playhouse he built at Carsehead for his and their neighbours' children.

There was also a cottage next to the rows with a barn they called 'the byre' and at first an old couple who kept hens lived there. After them, the next owners allowed the children to use the byre to put on wee concerts.
The children liked to play at the bing, would slide down on sleds, would make wee houses, taking along old bits of carpet. One of the mothers was good at telling stories and would have children in to tell them stories by firelight at night. The slaughterhouse was nearby and children would watch the animals being killed. They called it the 'killin hoose', but the girls would be sent away while boys were allowed to stay and watch. On slaughter days the burn ran red with animal blood.

When Elizabeth left school she started work in Fleming and Reid's Mill. She was very friendly with May Gallacher who happened to be my mother's cousin. Elizabeth and May used to pass each other notes in French while at their work.

As already mentioned, there was a shop in the first house in Furnace Row. There was also one in a house in Carsehead Row and Blair Store owned by Baird among the Peesweep rows. Elizabeth's father in-law was the manager of the Blair Store. During the General Strike, the miners raided the store and helped themselves to food. The leader was sitting on a crate in the middle of the shop directing proceedings, but he didn't realise that the crate was full of bottles of whisky which they left untouched. After the General Strike, the store never opened again and Mr Orr moved to work in a grocer shop in New Street.

Carsehead was a good distance from the shops in town, but vans came round selling goods including the Co-op grocer, Co-op Butcher, McClymont Butcher, and Hamilton hardware and paraffin.

When the houses were eventually condemned some people were reluctant to move, especially older people. The rents in the council houses they moved to were dearer, and some people struggled to pay them. If they

THE DALRY RAWS

Townend Street School building, later sorting office with post office attached. Photo by the author.

got too much into arrears they were evicted and had to find alternative privately rented houses.

People who were allocated four apartments [one living room and three bedrooms] mostly moved to Kirkland Crescent, but Elizabeth's family was allocated only a three apartment because her brothers had left home and her father had died, so they moved to Baidland Avenue.

When Elizabeth was a child, before she started school, she remembers watching a parade in the town when the school children paraded from the old school in Townend Street to the new Primary School on its opening day and her husband Hugh was in that parade. Townend Street School as it is today can be seen in photo of Townend Street School building.

Elizabeth and Hugh have two sons and she later worked as a classroom assistant in Dalry Primary School. At the time of writing they still live in Dalry in the new amenity houses next door to the school.

Kenneth Phillips

Kenneth has both a personal and professional interest in the raws. He was born in 1929 in 7 Peesweep Row (the 'Turned Raw'). His family moved out when he was weeks old, but his maternal uncle Dick Prasher continued to live at the raws, working as a miner. Dick was well known in Dalry for being well informed about local history, humorous poems, first aid, botany and birds. He was honoured with an OBE and MBE for weekly displays at Kelvingrove Museum. He later moved to a West Kilbride Road timber house and lost all his precious books when it burned down. Kenneth also had a great uncle who lived in Furnace Raw and he visited both relatives in

THE DALRY RAWS

Kenneth Phillips

the raws. There has been a family connection with the raws for a long time as old census records show ancestors named Lowe living in various raws. He also remembers there was a raw called the Long Raw. Stoopshill Raw tended to be separate from the other raws. He also remembers the raws at Borestone when he was a child and women doing their washing in the burn. In general, Catholics were housed at Borestone and originally mostly Protestants at Peesweep, although there were exceptions especially in more recent times.

His mother was brought up in the raws by her sister, (Kenneth's aunt Agnes) when her parents died. Kenneth's grandmother died when his mother was one year old and his grandfather died when she was seven. Her sixteen-years-old sister then took care of her while also working in the mill. His brother, Dick was called up on reaching the age of eighteen to serve in Ireland and another brother was called up to France in the First World War. There were another two older brothers also serving. Kenneth's uncle John was wounded by shrapnel six times. His uncle Andrew, when young, went to the nearby slaughterhouse and got free liver which would otherwise have been thrown away. Peesweep Raw was single ends and the rest were room and kitchens.

Kenneth remembers that in those days it was traditional for whole families dressed in their Sunday best to go for a walk after the church service up past the Peesweep, around the Loaning or through the Blair Estate whose gates were open on Sundays. Most of the men wore a small colourful scarf or 'grovat' (from the French cravat) around their neck. The Salvation Army and Brethren also held open air meetings near the Peesweep and one young cousin, hearing impassioned preaching outside, asked why they were swearing.

Several young children just starting school at the age of five died with Diphtheria and one possible explanation was a choked drain at St Palladius Primary School.

During the Second World War, Kenneth's sister, Catherine, was taken to Davidshill Hospital with Scarlet Fever.

Kenneth also remembers that during the war, a ship had managed to avoid the German submarines in the Atlantic and delivered a load of scarce fruit. The Co-op shop allocated one peach to each family in Dalry and Catherine was the only one who got it in their family.

Kenneth was good at maths and when he left school everyone said he should be an auditor. But, after the Second World War, it was decided there was a need for more sanitary inspectors and a vacancy came up for a County Council Sanitary Inspector. Two applied and he got the apprenticeship, based in Beith. Professionally he was familiar with the sanitary arrangements in the Peesweep Raws but not Borestone as it had been demolished by then.

There were no flush toilets in the raws and instead people had to relieve themselves in a dry closet which was a small toilet building with a board, not even a pail and no running water. Dry closets were shared by numerous households, often ten. There was also a midden, also called an ashpit. This was a small building with three sides and open on the fourth and people dumped their ashes out of the fire in there. The dry closets were also emptied into the ash pit so that human waste and ashes were mixed together. Once a year these were emptied by the farmer who had the right to them and spread on the fields as fertiliser. So long as the midden did not overflow it was not regarded as a health nuisance.

Kenneth's professional involvement with the raws included disagreements between neighbours such as over throwing out rubbish, but actually there was not a lot of rubbish because they burned most of it. There were not a lot of problems with the raws, but they lacked facilities. For example, the drainage was just a channel made of two bricks at an angle on the surface which allowed the water to run into the gutter.

There was one standpipe for each raw, one midden for each raw, one dry closet for each raw and there were ten houses in each raw.

Kenneth explained that the land and the raws were owned by the Blair Estate and Baird, the owner of the mining company. They were business associates. Baird owned the mines, but for every ton of coal taken out, Blair got a share. McCosh, the solicitor for Blair, was also solicitor for Baird.

In those days, the Sanitary Department of the County Council kept records on a card about every house. This listed resident members of the family and whether or not they were subtenants; whether there was overcrowding; medical conditions; whether anyone had TB, or whether the house was unfit. This information was used to decide which families were allocated a council house first.

Applicants for council houses were put on one of three separate lists – Unfit Houses, Overcrowded Houses and Subtenants. Priority on medical grounds only applied to Infective Pulmonary Tuberculosis. A fixed number of houses was allocated to each of the lists even if an unfit house was overcrowded and had a subtenant. All the houses in the raws were considered unfit. The length of time on the list decided who got the council house, usually counted from the date of marriage. With no house building for six years during the Second World War, some subtenants were still living with their parents and growing families for ten years and more. County councillors, Dr Alex Watt, and Peesweep resident, Bobby Hately, were consulted before each allocation.

When council houses were built and people started moving out of the raws to be rehoused, it was normal to put a closing order on the house in the raw they had left because it was assumed they were all unfit for habitation. But there was such a shortage of houses they were often re-let to a new family for a while until the whole raw was demolished. However sometimes a whole raw was rehoused simultaneously and this would allow for the raw to be demolished immediately after the tenants moved out. This happened when whole raws were rehoused simultaneously to the West Kilbride timber houses. Some tenants were reluctant to move out because they had lived in the raws for 50 years in some cases. The land used for building council houses was owned by Blair and Baird and the County Council had to buy it from them.

Kenneth married in 1959 and had three daughters. After working as a sanitary inspector and meat inspector he became a burgh surveyor, obtained a degree in civil engineering, was a civil engineer, municipal engineer and a lecturer in Glasgow College of Building and Printing. One of his hobbies was fishing and he acted as supervising engineer for the Auldmuir reservoir when it was acquired by Dalry Garnock Angling Club.

He now lives in Stewarton.

Robert Ward

Robert was born in 14 Turned Raw in 1931. He said that it was called that because originally it faced Blair Road but people say that when Captain Blair rode past in his pony and trap he didn't like to see the women sitting on their front step so the front doors were blocked up and the doors put on the back. He remembers Double Raw was back-to-back. His family later lived in 5 Furnace Raw. Stoopshill Raw was called the Big Raw. Robert remembers the McCrae family lived in number 1 Stoopshill Raw.

In Robert's family there were eight children and their mother and father but when they were in the raws some of the children hadn't been born yet. His mother was told after three children that she wouldn't be able to have any more, but then went on to have another five. Although there were never ten Ward family members resident in Turned Raw, it was still cramped in the single end. Robert said that it was a 'very wee room'. Robert's father was a stoker in the gasworks in a corner of what is now the public park. Because of the different ages of children coming and going at different times, and older children working different shifts, the door was never locked. Robert says he always played football. His mother would open the door and shout, 'Come in, Robert, yer dinner's ready!' Sometimes they had rabbit or pheasant which his father or older brothers had caught in a snare. Robert remembers his brothers gutting a bird and when one of his brothers smelled the 'guff' [stench] he had to go away and be sick.

Robert Ward

He remembers his mother washing in a big sink in front of the window in the wash house with a scrubbing board and the steam billowing round her. He would sneak up on her and give her a fright.

There was an outside coal house and outside toilets. About six families shared a toilet.

He said that if you needed the toilet in the middle of the night, you put your leg out the back window and went down the raw to the outside toilet in the pitch black. There were no torches.

Drinking water and water for cooking came from a pump in the middle of the raw. You took a pail and pumped the water. You got a bath in the wash house. Robert remembers when he was a wee boy his mother was giving him a bath in the wash house and he had put a towel up at the window because some of the window panes were broken. Some girls came up and poked a stick through to make the towel fall down so they could look in and he shouted at them. When adults were dressing and undressing in the same room as the children, the adults would tell the children to shut their eyes as there was little privacy.

He slept in a set-in bed with three brothers. They didn't have pillows but used a bolster because four children could share it more easily. Robert says despite all this, they were happy, happy days he spent in the raws. At Peesweep Raws, in fact in any raws, if you needed anything you got it, there was a great community spirit.

When Robert left school he got an apprenticeship with Nesbit's hairdresser and later set up his own barber's business. He also served in the army during the war.

One day when I was talking with Robert, his sister Margaret was there. She was born after the family left the raws, but she remembered visiting her granny who still lived there. She also remembered stories her mother told her about the raws. Margaret remembered visiting her granny and she would be standing with other women with their arms folded talking around the 'well' or pump. One day Margaret visited with four of her brothers and sisters and her granny gave them an orange between them. At the time she thought this was mean. Looking back now, she can see that her granny wouldn't have had much money or material goods. As she had around 50 grandchildren, she wouldn't have had enough to give them all as much as she might have liked. Margaret had the impression that the women in the raws spent all their time cooking and cleaning, 'it was a hard life.' Before Margaret was born her mother (Elizabeth or Leezie Ward) used to run a wee shop from her house to make some money. She bought pies and heated them and cooked dried peas. She would then put a plank of wood across two chairs to make a counter and sell the food. Neighbours would buy from her to save them having to go to the town for their own pies. She also sold sweeties in this way.

When the family left the raws they went to Lynn Avenue then Kirkland Crescent in the Timber Scheme.

[On reading Robert Ward's contribution, Kenneth Phillips commented that before Rab left school, he worked from the age of 11 at Hawhill farm and became excellent at hand milking the cows. There he met Kenny Phillips who was similarly employed at the neighbouring farms of Gowanlea and Hindog and they would compete with other schoolboys at lifting 28 lbs and 56 lbs above their head. Rab, despite being small and slight always won. It was a great surprise then, that when Robert left school, he got an apprenticeship with Nesbit's hairdresser.]

The Darling Houret Row

This poem or song was found among old photographs belonging to Robert Barr and may refer to the raws at Swinlees. (There is a farm there named South Houret). It appears to be anonymous.

I took a walk the other day down by the Hagsthorn Brae;
And many's the happy walk I've had, since first I went that way.
And down by David Littlejohn's across the burn did go;
Says I, while here my course I'll steer, to see the Houret Row.

So up the glen I gay went then, just gazing as I went;
To view the bonny flowery bank, where happy hours I spent.
But when the houses came in view, my tears began to flow;
For boys, it is the altered place, the Darling Houret Row.

While tears did drop, I never stopped, till I reached number 12;
Says I, 'I'm sure this is the door, where formerly I did dwell'.
But the houses are in ruins, I'm sorry to say so;
For boys, it is the altered place, the Darling Houret Row.

The Houret Row was once a place, you never would think long;
You'd either hear a good big lie, or a good old Irish song.
They had fiddlers and pipers, and music of all kinds;
And to carry on the sport I cashed many a big line.

The Houret Row was once inhabited, by darling Irish men;
And, on pay nights, they had their fights, no matter where or when.
They kept no jail, nor paid no bail, no police there did go;
If they showed their face, they were soon chased
From The Darling Houret Row.

On reading 'The Darling Houret Row', Kenneth Phillips provided the following information:
     Most of the farms around Dalry were owned by the Blair Estate and rented by the farmers. The estate employed a gamekeeper, Mr Wylie, who lived at the Houret. He was on duty 24 hours a day, seven days a week. As well as raising pheasants for the shooting season, he trapped foxes which raided hen houses, shot dogs worrying sheep, and chased poachers.
     Many miners trained greyhounds and gambled at the racetrack.

THE DALRY RAWS

After working hard underground all week, some enjoyed taking their greyhound over the hills in the fresh air around Dalry, searching for hares and the chase exercised both dog and man. Mr Wylie always carried a folded rifle over his arm and when he searched anyone and found a ferret, snares, nets, eggs of pheasants, partridges, grouse, ducks or peeweeps, they would be fined £2 at Kilmarnock Sheriff Court.

All the fishing rights belonged to the Blair Estate and members of the Dalry Garnock Angling Club were permitted to fish on the river Garnock and tributaries, except the Dusk and Bombo burns near Blair Castle. At that time trout were considered wild and it was not illegal to fish for them, but the landowner could order the fisherman off his land. Fishing for salmon on a Sunday was, and is still, illegal.

Conclusion

The oral histories confirm many aspects of the written history of miners' raws. For example, every respondent mentioned the lack of running water or electricity in the houses and the existence of separate wash houses in some cases. More than one mentioned the use of tar cloth on some roofs; storage of coal under the beds; set-in beds; overcrowding; unsurfaced outside paths; gardens and incidence of Diphtheria.

The respondents confirm each other's evidence in many cases. More than one person mentioned bathing in the wash house; gas lighting; visits from mobile shops; the golf course; a Carsehead resident who was disabled and walked with crutches; the fatal road accident of Myra Cairns; a neighbour who kept hens; the slaughter house; nearby Fleming and Reid's mill; the market garden in the Blair Estate; the Sunday School trip to the Blair Estate; shops run from houses; the story of how Turned Raw got its name; and the existence of the reading room. So much confirmation adds credence and authenticity, if any were needed, to their stories as accurate descriptions of life in the raws. There are also some minor contradictions between contributors and between them and other historic data I have been able to locate but these are minor and I believe they do not detract from the overall veracity of the book as a whole.

Many of the respondents knew each other and this is not surprising since their stays at the raws often overlapped. They also often mentioned the same neighbours. The tables on the following page, 'Years of respondents' connection with the raws' illustrates the lengths of stay or when they visited and any overlap.

Physical surroundings

All the respondents described in detail the arrangements for obtaining water, perhaps because that is the biggest contrast between housing in the raws and modern housing. It is hardly surprising that water received so much attention since it is of course a basic requisite for life and fetching it must have taken up a lot of time and effort every day. More than one respondent described how the scullery at Peesweep contained a bucket of clean water and how dirty water was emptied into an outside uncovered sink. At Peesweep drainage was supplied by forming a line of pairs of bricks placed at an angle on the surface of the ground which allowed water to run into the gutter. At Carsehead there was an inside sink for storing water

THE DALRY RAWS

Tables showing the period during which each interviewee was connected with the Raws.

CARSEHEAD

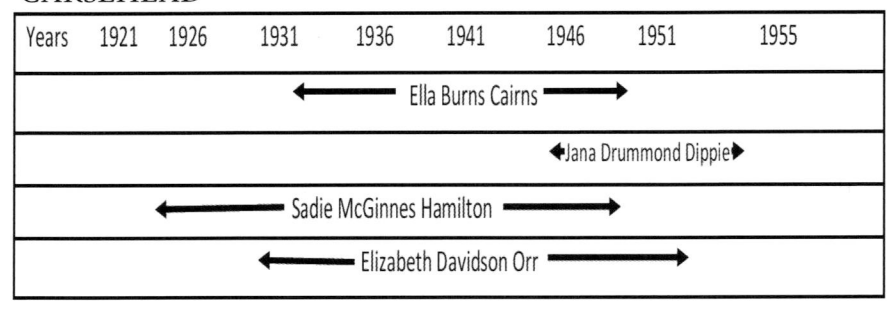

Years	1921	1926	1931	1936	1941	1946	1951	1955
			←——— Ella Burns Cairns ———→					
						←Jana Drummond Dippie→		
		←——— Sadie McGinnes Hamilton ———→						
			←——— Elizabeth Davidson Orr ———→					

PEESWEEP

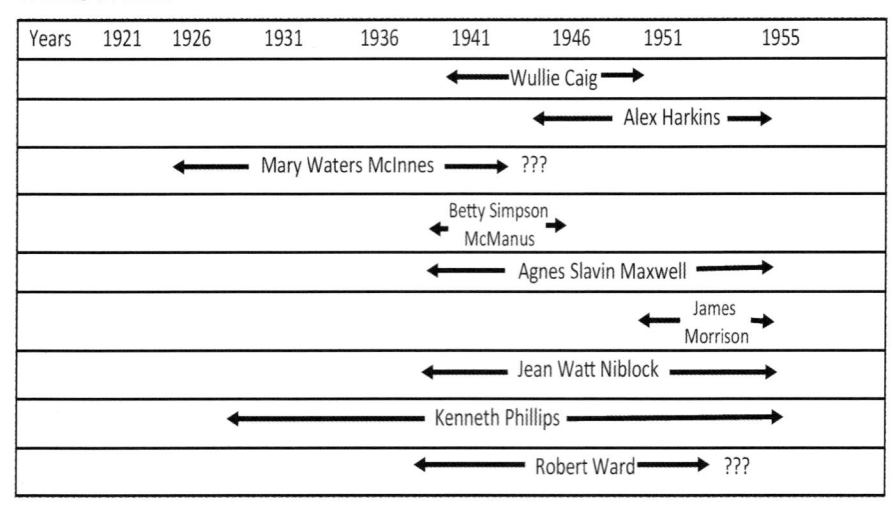

Years	1921	1926	1931	1936	1941	1946	1951	1955
						←—Wullie Caig—→		
							←——Alex Harkins——→	
		←——— Mary Waters McInnes ———→ ???						
					Betty Simpson ← → McManus				
					←——— Agnes Slavin Maxwell ———→			
							←—James Morrison—→	
				←——— Jean Watt Niblock ———→				
		←——————— Kenneth Phillips ———————→						
				←——— Robert Ward ———→ ???				

136

brought from the pump and a sink for emptying dirty water.

They also described the management of activities requiring water, such as washing clothes, bathing and going to the toilet, especially at night. Some people described the use of a potty and some described climbing out the window to go to the closet during the night. The respondent who worked as a sanitary inspector was a fund of information on the removal of human waste from areas not connected to sewage facilities. Some respondents from Peesweep remembered outside flush toilets and others did not. All of the Carsehead respondents remembered outside flush toilets.

Several people described the arrangements for following a rota for use of the wash houses where they existed as well as the ritual of setting and lighting a fire under the boiler to heat the water for washing clothes. Some respondents' descriptions of wash day were very striking. For example, one described his mother washing clothes in a big sink in front of a window using a scrubbing board while steam billowed round her and another described playing in the suds on the floor.

One respondent mentioned the raws at Borestone and remembered the women washing clothes in the burn there. A few people mentioned the difficulty of drying clothes in front of the fire in wet weather.

Most people also mentioned the lack of electricity and the cooking of food, again hardly surprising since ranges, trivets over open fires and gas cookers with low pressure made a necessary human requirement so much harder then.

The physical structure of the houses was not described so much, perhaps because most of the respondents were children and may not have noticed any structural problems but dampness was mentioned in the description of marks on the ceiling and how shoes left under the bed would be damp when retrieved.

Despite these privations, respondents described how families made the raws as homely as possible and they could describe the furniture, curtains, linoleum and rugs, decoration, housework, practices such as the removal of shoes before going inside, cultivation of gardens and whitening of outside steps. Removal of ranges and installation of coal fires was mentioned as was installation of modern amenities such as gas cookers. A few people described how some families removed one of the set-in beds to make a small scullery.

At an earlier period in raws history, the *Ardrossan and Saltcoats Herald* of 19 September 1863 reported on the first annual horticultural show of the Blair Works Horticultural Society, held in the works school room. As well as the usual competitions for the best vegetables and flowers there was a competition for the best kept house in the rows at Blair Works. Mrs H. Beveridge won for Blair and Mrs J. White won for Carsehead and Linn.

THE DALRY RAWS

All of these paint a picture of people working hard to make their families comfortable. Perhaps Agnes Maxwell summed it up best when she said, 'The houses were not slums.'

Physical Surroundings – overcrowding

The legal definition of housing overcrowding varies over time and place. The literature provides definitions concerning floor area per person and takes account of the age and sex of the residents. There are definitions as to what constitutes a bedroom which I believe some of the bedrooms described by residents would fail. Perhaps the simplest rule of thumb is that there should be a minimum of one room for every two people. This is not a demanding requirement as nowadays most council housing departments aim to provide three rooms for four people and four rooms where siblings are of different sexes and over ten years old. The oral histories reveal that only two families had a minimum of a room for every two people. The rest were overcrowded by this definition. Overcrowding was officially recognised as a problem in the raws and considered when allocating council houses.

I revisited the fourteen census sheets I had used before to calculate that the average occupancy in Peesweep over 50 years was 5.4 people per house. My aim was to find out the average occupancy per room. I discovered that in single ends the average number of people per room was 4.7 and in room and kitchens it was 3.8. This gave an average occupancy per room of 3.99 - nearly double the modern minimum.

Many people described sleeping arrangements which allowed large numbers of people to sleep in one or two rooms, such as set-in beds, hurley beds and chairs which could be folded out into beds. Up to four children slept in one bed using bolsters instead of pillows because they were easier to share. One respondent said that the usual arrangement was for the parents and the youngest child to sleep in the kitchen and all the other children in the room.

Another respondent said that if all the residents were in the house simultaneously it made routine household activities such as baking impossible.

As well as making life difficult inside, overcrowding increased the pressure on shared facilities outside, especially toilets. There is a lack of consensus among respondents as to how many families shared a toilet in Peesweep shortly before demolition; the estimates of the respondents range from five to ten but if we assume the smallest number is accurate, bearing in mind that the average number of residents in each house was around 5.4, that means that 27 people probably shared one toilet. The consensus is that by that time, at Carsehead, two families shared a flush toilet which is better than at Peesweep but still gives an average of nearly eleven people sharing.

Two residents stated that there were flush toilets at Peesweep.

The evidence submitted to the Royal Commission earlier in 1913 indicates that the proportion of houses to toilets varied between 2.3 houses per toilet to 5.75 houses per toilet, or a range of 12 to 31 people, giving an average number of households sharing each toilet as 3.6 households or nearly twenty people. I considered whether the number of toilets provided for rows of room and kitchens might be higher than for single ends to take account of the former being able to accommodate more people, but this was not the case. This situation had improved by the time the interviewees lived at the raws, especially considering that by that time at Carsehead, flush toilets shared by two families had been installed. From a twenty-first century point of view one wonders at the thinking of the owners when toilets were being planned and installed. The proportion of toilets to houses seems to have been randomly decided, the overriding consideration presumably being to keep costs as low as possible. This reveals a lack of respect, if not downright antipathy towards the residents from owners and managers who became rich by exploiting the miners who risked their lives at work and paid for the privilege of living in the substandard houses the owners saw fit to provide. We can be confident in assuming that the owners did not share a toilet with people from another family.

HEALTH

All but one of the respondents were born before the establishment of the National Health Service in 1948 and some could remember families contributing to private health insurance schemes which predated the National Health Service. Midwifery services were available before the commencement of the NHS, as was dentistry, at least tooth extraction.

Contrary to commonly held beliefs, free hospital treatment was available prior to 1948 as evidenced by oral history contributors describing children being treated for Scarlet Fever or Diphtheria in Davidshill Hospital or Irvine Central Hospital. One resident also described having a tonsillectomy in Seafield Hospital, Ayr, in 1936. For more specialised medical treatment after the inauguration of the NHS, people could be treated at more distant hospitals such as Killearn.

Unfortunately, the treatment for Diphtheria available at that time, prior to the widespread availability of Penicillin, was basic and many children died despite hospitalisation, including one respondent's sister. Separation of infectious children, however, was effective to a certain extent in controlling spread of the disease, as was fumigation of the houses where residents had been affected.

The other common communicable disease was Tuberculosis and Ayrshire County Council Sanitary Department kept records of the houses where the disease affected residents. Tuberculosis is a disease associated with poor housing. Overcrowding, poor air quality as a result of inadequate ventilation, and the presence of mould and smoke can increase the incidence of Tuberculosis.

In living memory, and prior to the discovery of many modern medicines, people relied on herbal remedies such as provided by one respondent's grandmother.

The respondents' experience of health provision may have varied depending on whether they were born before or after the inauguration of the NHS.

Employment

As already mentioned, although the raws were built for miners and their families, by the end of their occupation, the proportion of miners had dwindled greatly, although several respondents mentioned their grandfathers having been miners in Dalry. One respondent's father had been a miner in a barytes mine in Lochwinnoch and one's husband had been a coal miner in Dalry.

Occupations held by respondents, their family members and neighbours were very varied, and many people changed career throughout their lives. Miners sometimes changed to a less demanding job when they were near retirement, such as surface work or road sweeper. One respondent described how three uncles emigrated to America to seek employment outwith mining.

Some people became self-employed shop keepers, selling products from their home.

Many worked in manufacturing especially brickworks, steelworks, gasworks, explosives and dyeworks and one or two worked on the railway. Others worked in services such as shops, the golf course, catering, hairdressing, tailoring, street sweeping, chimney sweeping, domestic service and park keeping.

A few mentioned agricultural or horticultural work including seasonal work picking berries at the Blair Estate. One respondent's father was the supervisor in the slaughterhouse.

The armed forces were also mentioned, sometimes war interrupting early jobs or apprenticeships.

Two went onto professional careers in teaching and college lecturing. One of the Carsehead residents was a violin teacher. One person's uncle, Richard Prasher, an ex-miner, and resident of the raws in earlier years, received an MBE in 1979 for Services to the Environment in the West of Scotland.

Residents of the raws who became well known

Hugh Caig was born in Peesweep Row in 1893. (He was Wullie Caig's grandfather.) He was a professional footballer with Middlesborough F. C. for a time.

Alexander Young Malcolmson was born at Peesweep in 1865 and emigrated to America when he was fifteen. He worked in a grocery shop then bought a small grocery business. He then started dealing in coal, eventually owning six depots in 1902. Henry Ford asked him to bankroll a new automotive company and together they formed Ford and Malcolmson, allowing Ford to design the Model A. In the first year the company made over $250 000 profit. He parted company with Ford and returned to dealing in coal, coke and building supplies. When he died in 1929, aged 64 he was estimated to have amassed $2 000 000.

Richard (Dick) Prasher was born in Peesweep Row in 1899. He was honoured in the Queen's New Year Honours list of 1979 by being awarded Member of the Order of the British Empire (MBE) for services to the environment in the West of Scotland. This was in recognition of his work in providing regular natural history displays in Kelvingrove Museum.

Robert Tait was born at Barkip / The Den in 1874 and moved to Lanarkshire with his family when still young. He started working in mining at age 11 but later had a book of poems published entitled *Rustic Songs of Nature*. They have been recognised as similar in style and subjects to those of Robert Burns.

The occupation which was mentioned most often, even more than mining, was mill work in Fleming and Reid's woollen mill. A large number of local girls started work there when they left school and one woman described putting her name down at age fourteen when someone from the mill visited the school shortly before she left. A few women mentioned giving up work when they became pregnant. No-one mentioned being required to leave work when they married although this 'marriage bar' existed in Britain from the 1900s until the passing of the Sex Discrimination Act in 1975. Not every employer operated a marriage bar but often they did not have to enforce it because women themselves chose to leave work on marriage or becoming pregnant.

Only one mentioned unemployment when it took her husband a while to find alternative employment when he wanted to leave the mine, but even he eventually found work in Broadlie brickworks.

Three respondents mentioned working part time before they left school. Many of the jobs mentioned were typical for children, such as milk or newspaper delivery, but one mentioned running a snooker room. Two mentioned having part-time jobs when they were twelve years old, not very unusual when the school leaving age was fourteen, but one person described selling ice cream when he was at primary school. This may strike us as surprising nowadays but literature can put a different complexion on it.

'In the modern world, school education has become so central to society that schoolwork has become the dominant work for most children, often replacing participation in productive work.'

'Work is undertaken from an early age by vast numbers of children in the world and may have a natural place in growing up. Work can contribute to the well-being of children in a variety of ways; children often choose to work to improve their lives, both in the short- and long-term. At the material level, children's work often contributes to producing food or earning income that benefits themselves and their families; and such income is especially important when the families are poor…Young people often enjoy their work, especially paid work, … children often find ways to combine their work with play.'

(c.f. https://en.wikipedia.org/wiki/Child_labour#Potential_positives)

Whether it was legal to employ such a young child is another matter. Since the nineteenth century there have been Acts of Parliament making it illegal to employ children under certain ages in mines and factories. There are local by-laws governing the employment of children in work such as milk and newspaper delivery. The Children and Young Persons (Scotland) Act 1937 states that 'no child shall engage or be employed in street trading'. This seems to outlaw selling ice cream outside as described, no matter the child's age. This does not mean that it did not happen.

Household Economy

Most of the interviewees mentioned money being scarce and how this impacted on them, for example being expected to eat all their food; fruit being a treat which had to be shared; residents giving soup to others who were less well off; shortage of money due to illness or disability; only one room being heated; eating simple cheap food like porridge, soup and saps; concern that they might not be able to afford council house rents; receiving free liver from the slaughterhouse; and children taking part time jobs from a young age.

Many respondents mentioned money-saving or money-making activities such as making quilts from old dresses; making clothes; building bicycles from scrap metal; collecting fallen wood to use for kindling; catching rabbits in snares; keeping hens; or running small shops from their house. One was honest about residents stealing food, but never from each other. In fact, there was a culture of sharing food and respondents described sharing home-grown vegetables, home-cooked food and rabbits and pheasants acquired by poaching as well as stolen vegetables from farmers' fields.

However, the lives of the residents in the raws were not totally confined by lack of money. Some could afford to take part in the arts through violin lessons and competitive Highland Dancing. Pigeon fancying was another pastime requiring financial outlay.

Law and Order
As already mentioned, several people described the theft of vegetables from farmers' fields especially during the miners' strike and one mentioned it happening at other times but only because the people in the raws 'had nothing'. Poaching seems to have been common in some families. The same person mentioned theft of chickens from a farm and of coal from the brickworks. There was also a description of the tossing school with people acting as lookouts in case the police appeared.

On the other hand, nearly everyone mentioned loyalty and support between neighbours and the practice of leaving doors unlocked because of the absence of theft. It is more disturbing to learn that one respondent was aware of domestic violence occurring in a neighbour's household.

Dalry
As well as describing the raws, respondents mentioned many facts about Dalry in the past and these descriptions provide a picture of Dalry which is different in many ways from today.

For example, one person remembered horse-drawn carts, bringing goods from Glasgow, stopping at the ford in the Rye water to drink. This was near the cottage hospital or 'seik hoose' next to the bridge at the entrance to the public park. Along with Davidshill Hospital this meant that Dalry had two hospitals.

Some people might also be surprised to learn that Dalry had a golf course between Peesweep and the Blair Estate as well as two tennis courts in the public park.

During the Second World War there was an internment camp for Italians at Tofts.

There was a lodging house for vulnerable single men at Drakemyre. There was a market garden in the Blair Estate (where peacocks roamed the grounds) as well as a working smithy near the South Lodge.

When most of the respondents were very young the only council houses were at Townend Street, Lynn Avenue, Merksworth Avenue and Garnock Street. Where most of the Blair scheme, Lynn scheme and West Kilbride (Timber) scheme are now, there were farmers' fields.

Where there were streetlights they were fuelled by gas, not electricity and there was a gasworks in the public park.

The Post Office sorting office was once a school.

There were many businesses, that are now closed, including Carsehead Brickworks, the slaughterhouse, Paterson's buses and the creamery on Blair Road across from the railway station. Interviewees mentioned retail businesses now closed such as Loudon's and Knowles's chemists, Cochrane's newsagent, Hannah's shoe shop and McClymont's and Marshall's butchers. Numerous mobile shops travelled round the town including various Co-op vans; Wullie Hamilton's paraffin and hardware; Ramages fruit van; ice cream tricycle and McClymont's butcher's van.

SOCIAL RELATIONSHIPS, NEIGHBOURS AND FRIENDS

All respondents mentioned relationships between the people who lived in the raws. Many described communal activities such as groups of children going swimming together; playing football; sledging on tin trays; and co-operating to put on concerts for the adults. There were also joint outings to the seashore.

Two of the respondents in the oral history referred to the reading room; one explicitly and the other less clearly. They said that it was a building where retired miners could go to socialise and it could also be used for celebrations such as wedding receptions. Many raws in other parts of Ayrshire had 'institutes' which provided a meeting room, a library and a games room. These appeared to be much more substantial than the reading room at Peesweep which consisted of two single ends. Institutes were donated by mine owners or benefactors and were particularly prominent in remote raws such as at Cronberry. One can imagine that these remote villages had great need of a community space since they were outwith walking distance of other social provision. As already stated, Peesweep and Carsehead were not very isolated and residents were within walking distance of several private libraries, a public hall and various church halls, not to mention public houses. An argument could be made that Peesweep and Carsehead did not therefore need an institute and perhaps the reading room was a gesture towards providing a space for the exclusive use of miners and their families without going to the expense of building an institute which may have been perceived as unnecessary by the owners.

Young women travelled together to and from their work at Fleming and Reid's Mill and older married women operated a rota for use of the wash houses; stood around the water pump or sat on the front steps blethering; worked together to complete major house-working tasks on the same day, such as washing bed boards and blankets; and gave food such as soup to neighbours who needed it.

Men took groups of children on long walks to the coast; walked together on a Sunday; built playthings for the children; and shared food, especially during the miners' strike.

Family relationships were strong and different generations of families often stayed near each other with grandparents described as regularly having grandchildren to stay. There were occasions when older sisters took on responsibility for younger siblings if their parents died. Sometimes a family took in a neighbour who was not related to them. This sort of kindness to others extended to people from outwith the raws as exemplified by Agnes's grandmother taking in people who were new to the town until they found a place of their own. Another example is residents giving food and money to people from the lodging house.

All in all, the impression received is of a close-knit community in the raws, with neighbours knocking and entering each other's houses without waiting for the door to be answered.

There were many examples of people helping each other and lending or giving material goods.

Although it was part of one person's job to resolve disagreements about sanitary arrangements among residents, actually there were very few. Another person, however, said that there was always fighting at the Turned Raw.

I have a sense of life in the raws being lived collectively with front doors open and neighbours spending a large part of their time together. One respondent said that if a neighbour's door was not opened by a certain time in the morning, someone would go and check that everything was alright.

It would be noted if a doctor called and when s/he left a neighbour would call in to offer to help if needed, for example taking a prescription to the chemist.

Social cohesion was perhaps strengthened by antipathy experienced from some people outwith the raws. Several respondents mentioned town people looking down on them because of erroneous ideas about sanitary arrangements and living space in the raws. There was rivalry between town people and some raws people about who should be allocated council houses first and a belief that ex-miners experienced prejudice when looking for work outwith mining.

Some of the respondents drew attention to the religious and racial prejudice that was prevalent at the time when some Catholics who had originally come from Ireland felt that they were not wanted by local Protestant residents. One person mentioned being discouraged to associate with Catholics.

The residents were very loyal to the other people in their raws, although there was a lack of social interaction between Carsehead and Peesweep residents. This could sometimes spill over into antipathy when some Carsehead residents used insulting terms to describe Peesweep residents, characterising them as undesirable because many were Irish Catholics.

All of the respondents however mentioned how their close neighbours helped each other in numerous ways and many said that the best thing about the raws was the neighbourliness. Although many described their new council houses as being bigger and seeming to be

THE DALRY RAWS

luxurious compared to the raws, they nearly all said that they missed the friendliness and community of the raws.

    'A little among neighbours is worth more than riches in a wilderness.'
-Welsh Proverb.

Appendix 1

List of the names of all householders at Peesweep and Carsehead Rows, recorded in the 1885 valuation roll. (Note that the original was handwritten and parts were difficult to decipher so there may be some inaccuracies.)

PEESWEEP

Double Row:
John McCluckie, Bricklayer
James McCulloch, Pitman
Jas McKessock, Pitheadman
John Smith, Miner
John Gemmell, Miner
James Brown, Miner
John Lennon(?), Labourer
William Ray, Miner
William Lowe, Miner
James Simpson, Labourer
James Wallace, Miner
Margaret (Hill?) or Murray, Widow
Isaac Cary, Miner
Henry Barbour, Miner
Andrew Welsh, Pitman
Richard Jackson, Pitman
James Quin, Pitman
Robert Jackson, Pitman
John McAllister, Miner
Hugh Robertson, Miner
John Gordon, Charfiller
John Wallace, Miner
David McManus, Miner
James Hill, Pitman
Henry Hawthorn, Miner
Michael Martin, Miner
Thomas Hill, Pitman
Robert Crawford, Charfiller
Hugh Killochan, Charfiller
Thomas McBride, Miner
John Rice, Pitman

THE DALRY RAWS

Patrick Lennon, Charfiller
John McKillop, Miner
William McKinnon

Furnace Row:
William O'Maulie, Miner
John Morning, Miner
Thomas Crawford, Miner
John Dunn, Driver
James Jackson, Miner
Thomas Stein, Miner
Thomas Brannigan, Miner
Henry McLuskie, Miner
James McIlhenney, Pitman
James Hand, Pitman
John McNeish, Miner
James Berry, Miner
John Moore, Miner
John Young, Riddler
James Criely, Miner
John Ward, Miner
Hugh Clifford, Miner
Daniel McGill, Miner
Hamilton Campbell, Miner
Jane McGimpsey/McLeod, Widow

Peesweep Row:
Robert Ferguson, Labourer
Edward Hawthorn, Miner
William Lang, Miner
James Andrews, Miner
Henry Mitchell, Miner
David Murray, Miner
William McCarle, Miner
James Blackley, Miner
James Doolan, Charfiller
John McCarle, Charfiller
John Crealy, Miner
John Kilpatrick, Pitman
James Watson, Miner
Neil Cain, Pitman
John Grogan, Miner
William Purdie, Miner

THE DALRY RAWS

George Rankine, Miner
William Allan, Charfiller
David Morrow, Engineman
David Nesbit, Pitman
David Black, Miner
William Smith, Miner
Hugh Mooney, Miner
Robert McLuskie, Labourer

Single Row:
William Dempsey, Miner
Elizabeth Smith / Moore, Widow
John Hendry, Miner
John Gray, Pitman
Hamilton Kilpatrick, Pitman
David Close, Miner
Peter McBride, Miner
Thomas Gray, Miner
David Gemmell, Miner
Thomas Devlin, Riddler
Thomas Dempster, Miner
George Stevens, Miner
John McGimpsey, Miner
Joseph Shannon, Miner
James Carley, Charfiller
Ann Jane Evans / Blair, Widow
James Gallocher, Miner
Charles ? , Miner
James Caig, Miner
James Kennedy, Miner
William Stevens, Pitman
Nathaniel Murray, Miner
Peter Black, Miner

Foreman's Row:
George Davison, Miner
Robert Brown, Engineman
John Weir, Oversman
Andrew Pringle, Engineman
Hugh Ramsay, Engineer
John Murphy, Miner
John McBlane, Engineman
James Mackie, Oversman

THE DALRY RAWS

Jane Cochrane/Bennie, Widow
William Young, Pitheadman

CARSEHEAD

Carsehead Old Row:
George Boyle, Miner
John McDonald, Miner
William Walker, Pitman
John Roddie, Miner
James Hill, Miner
William Hill, Miner
John Smith, Carter
William Perry, Miner
Robert Brownlie, Pitman
Adam Lorrimer, Miner
Archibald Harkins (?), Miner
John Morron (?), Miner
William Houston, Miner
John McNeish, Pitman
Robert Irvine, Miner
John Hay, Miner
William Chalmers, Miner
James Armstrong, Miner
William Baird, Labourer
John Gourlay, Pitman
Robert McDonald, Miner
James Brownlie, Pitman
John Snodgrass, Pitman
Robert Heely, Miner
Robert Lindsay, Miner
Andrew Allan, Pitman
James Houston, Miner
Thomas Fullerton, Miner
John Brodie, Blacksmith
David Watson, Miner
George Andrews, Miner
Dobbin Paterson, Miner
John Kennedy, Miner

New Row:
James Cummings, Miner
Andrew Marley, Miner

THE DALRY RAWS

George Marley, Miner
Robert Gibson, Miner
James Reid, Charfiller
William Hay, Miner
Samuel Welsh, Railway Signalman
William Johnson (?), Charfiller
John Sloan, Miner
John Devlin, Miner
Thomas Gilmour, Pitman
George Marlie, Miner
Edward Morgan, Miner
Robert McMurdo, Miner
Andrew Smith, Pitman
John Wallace, Miner
John Keary, Miner
Ephraim Tosh (?), Miner
Robert Sloan, Ironfounder
James McCallum, Miner
Alexander McBride, Miner
Thomas Hay, Miner
John Dunn, Pitman
Agnes Miller or Gunn, widow
William Boyce, Miner
James Wallace, Miner
Robert Kennedy, Miner
James Murray, Miner
John McCallum, Miner
William Sloan, Miner
Robert Hawthorn, Miner
William Nicol, Miner

GLOSSARY OF MINING OCCUPATIONS MENTIONED ABOVE:

Charfiller - filled wagons, trucks, etc., with calcined ironstone, using shovel.
Driver - leads ponies used for hauling loads, often on rails.
Engineman - drove a haulage engine; a winding engineman or winder drove the winding engine.
Oversman/overman - the foreman or senior underground official of a pit, ran the whole of the underground workings in the management's absence. The overman was responsible for production or output. There was generally one overman for each shift.
Pitheadman - worked the headgear at the pit head of a mine.
Pitman - inspected and repaired the shafts, including descending the shaft

THE DALRY RAWS

on top of the cage, visually checking for problems.
Riddler - Operated sieve for separating large minerals from small.

Appendix 2

List of the names of all householders at Peesweep and Carsehead Rows, recorded in the 1948 Valuation Roll.

PEESWEEP

NEW DOUBLE ROW:
Thomas McCrae, Labourer
George Hall
Jeanie Sanders
John Fleck
Elizabeth Caig
Robert McCallan, Collier
Andrew Hailley, Collier
John Gordon junior, Boiler Fireman
Robert Kirk, Labourer
Elizabeth Blackwood
Hugh McCalmont, Brickworker
Thomas Andrews, Collier
Catherine McCann
John Rae, Labourer
James Skeoch, Labourer
Elizabeth Thomson
Jeanie Davidson
Lochy Galloway, Dynamite Worker

FURNACE ROW:
Helen Skeoch
George B Thomson, Labourer
James McInnes, Miner
Elizabeth Clark
William Welsh, Labourer
James Simpson, Collier
Elizabeth McManus
Jeanie Harkins
Patrick Higgins, Labourer

THE DALRY RAWS

Thomas Dunlop, Collier
John McGill, Labourer
Alexander Beattie, Labourer
William Ward, Collier
Hugh Aird, Washerman
Charles McGill, Labourer
John Harvey, Surfaceman
William Lowe, Miner
James Morrison, Labourer
Mary Skinner, Mill worker
Abram Wales, Engineer
William Rose, Collier
Robert Hately, Labourer
William Townsley

Peesweep Row:
James Gordon, Labourer
William Orr, Labourer
Mary G Wilson
James Wallace, Collier
James Andrew, Labourer
Jane McFarlane, Weaver
Richard Prasher, Labourer
Thomas Shaw, Collier
Joseph Houston
George Berryman, Labourer
Robert Tait, Labourer
Robert Andrews

New Single Row:
William Long, Labourer
David Cooper, Collier
Robert Wallace, Collier
Robert McCallum, Collier
Annie Brownlie
Annie Flanagan
John Roddie, Labourer
Robert Nelson, Labourer
Hugh Long, Roadsman

THE DALRY RAWS

James Crawford, Bricklayer
Alexander Kane, Labourer
William Simpson, Labourer
James Gallacher, Labourer
Annie Murray
William Lowe
William Caig, Grocer
James Murray, Labourer
Christina Reid
Archibald Harkins
Isaac Wales, Labourer
Robert Ward, Brickworker
Alexander Higgins, Collier
Mary McBride
Hugh Robinson, Collier
Peter Friels, Labourer
William Ward, Labourer
Thomas Lindsay
James Morrison, Labourer

Foreman's Row:
Robert Aird, Wright
James Carroll, Miner
Thomas Ward, Labourer
Robert Crawford, Fireman
Hugh Caig, Miner
Catherine Welsh
Annie A Murray
Robert Carswell, Pitheadman
William Kirk, Pitheadman
Sarah Friels
Catherine Robertson

CARSEHEAD

Carsehead Old Row:
Robert Millar, Labourer
Catherine Stirling
James Chapman, Surfaceman

THE DALRY RAWS

Agnes Davidson
Arthur Hill
Jean Borland
Mary Ann Houston
William Cairns, Collier
William Houston
William Dunn, Labourer
Alexander Houston, Miner
William McInnes, Miner
John Anderson, Collier
John Lindsay, Miner
Neil Millan, Collier
Isabella Cox
Sarah McGinnes
Mary Miller
James Miller, Collier
Michael McMeekin
James Caig, Miner
Robert Paterson, Collier
James Houston, Miner
William Marley, Miner
John Andrews, Collier
Alexander Roddie, Miner
Henry Millar, Collier
William Anderson, Collier
Thomas Morgan, Labourer
Mathilda Burns
William Garret, Labourer
George Harvie, Labourer
Mary Rae
Mary McClure

Sources

Bagworth H J, (1998) *The Role of Agents, Visitors and Inspectors in The Development of Elementary Education 1826 – 1870*, PhD Thesis, Brunel University.
Beatty C, Fothergill S, Gore T. (2019) *The State of the Coalfields 2019, Economic and social conditions in the former coalfields of England, Scotland and Wales. A report commissioned by the Coalfields Regeneration Trust.*
Bohata K, Jones A, Mantin M, Thompson S. (2020) *Disability in Industrial Britain. A Cultural and Literary History of Impairment in the Coal Industry, 1880–1948,* Manchester University Press, whole book available at https://www.ncbi.nlm.nih.gov/books/NBK553580/
Bolton W S. (2007) *Black Faces and Tackety Boots*. Self-published.
Bowen C S C; Sellar A C. (1871) *Second Report of the Commissioners appointed to inquire into the Truck System Report presented to both Houses of Parliament*. HMSO.
Bremner D. (undated) *Extract From 'The Industries of Scotland',* http://www.scottishmining.co.uk/397.html
Brown J & McKerrell T. (1979) *Ayrshire Miners' Rows. Evidence submitted to the Royal Commission On Housing In Scotland.* Ayrshire Archaeological and Natural History Society (AANHS)
Campbell R H. (original date of publication unknown) *The Iron Industry in Ayrshire,* excerpt printed by (AANHS)
Clark E. (2015) *Sanny Sloan, The Miners' MP and His Family of the First World War*
https://en.wikisource.org/wiki/Dictionary_of_National_Biography,_1885-1900/Baird,_James
Hawksworth C. (2020) *A History of Benslie and Fergushill.* Self-published
Hilditch S. (22 January 2014) *Housing the Key Achievement of the First Labour Government,* www.redbrickblog.co.uk.
Hutton G. (2001) *Scottish Black Diamonds.* Stenlake Publishing, Catrine Ayrshire.
https://www.irish-genealogy-toolkit.com/Irish-immigration-to-Britain.html
McGeorge A. (1875) *Bairds of Gartsherrie*. Privately Printed.

Macdonald CR. (1912) *County of Ayr Public Health Annual Report.* Ayrshire County Council.
MacGregor M, Lee GW & Wilson GV (1920) *The Iron Ores of Scotland.* HMSO
Maclure J. Stuart (Editor) (1965) *Educational Documents 1816 to The Present Day.* Routledge
Miller E. (1980) *Comparative Study of the Development of Mining Trade Unions, Ayrshire*, unpublished dissertation
Miller J. (Spring 1998) *The Raws.* Largs and District Family History Society Newsletter
https://www.mindat.org
Paxman J. (2021) *Black Gold.* Collins
https://railscot.co.uk
Royal Commission on the Housing of the Industrial Population of Scotland. (1918) Report, HMSO
https://scotlandspeople.gov.uk
https://scotlandsplaces.gov.uk/digital-volumes/ordnance-survey-name-books/ayrshire-os-name-books-1855-1857/ayrshire-volume-20
Scottish Mining Website. (undated) *Biographies & Obituaries, James Baird.* http://www.scottishmining.co.uk/386.html
Scottish Mining Website. (undated) *Extracts from 'Mining District Report 1859'.* http://www.scottishmining.co.uk/119.html
Scottish Mining Website. (undated) *Miners' Housing In Scotland. Extracted from Chapter XIV Report of Royal Commission on the Housing of the Industrial Population of Scotland, 1918* http://www.scottishmining.co.uk/Indexes/housing.html
Sinclair J B. (1791–1845) *The Statistical Account of Scotland. Drawn up from the communications of the ministers of the different parishes*, W Creech. Edinburgh,
Sleight G E. (1966) *Ayrshire Coalmining and Ancillary Industries.* AANHS
Strawhorn J. (1979) *A Postscript to the facsimile 'Ayrshire Miners' Rows'.* AANHS
Strawhorn J. (1975) *Ayrshire – The Story of a County*, AANHS
Terris I. (2001) *Twenty Years Down The Mines*, Stenlake
Turner A. & McIvor A. T*he Scottish Historical Review*, October 2017. Volume XCVI, 2: No. 243: 187–213 "Bottom dog men": Disability, Social Welfare and Advocacy in the Scottish Coalfields in

the Interwar Years, 1918–1939

Ward J. T. (1969) *Ayrshire Landed Estates in the 19th Century.* AANHS

Whatley C A. (1983) *The Finest Place for a Lasting Colliery.* AANHS

Wilson G M. (1977) *The miners of the West of Scotland and their trade unions, 1842-74.* PhD thesis. http://theses.gla.ac.uk/2112/.

Acknowledgements

I am very grateful to the people who agreed to be interviewed for the oral histories. Thank you, Wullie Caig, Ella Burns Cairns, Jana Drummond Dippie, Alex Harkins, Sadie Hamilton McGinnes, Mary Waters McInnes, Betty Simpson McManus, Agnes Slavin Maxwell, James Morrison, Jean Watt Niblock, Elizabeth Davidson Orr, Kenneth Phillips, Jock Porter, Robert Ward, and George Young.

Thanks are also due to the following people who read the work at various stages and made helpful suggestions: Dick Graham, Evelyn Grassick, Chris Hawksworth, Eileen Herteis, Martin Kostigovs, Charlie McGurk, Mary Rose Martin, Linda Storie, and Douglas Woolf.

Thanks are also due to the people who permitted use of their photographs.